Open Ukraine

Changing Course towards a European Future

Edited by
Taras Kuzio and Daniel Hamilton

Center for Transatlantic Relations
Paul H. Nitze School of Advanced International Studies
Johns Hopkins University

Kuzio, Taras and Daniel S. Hamilton, *Open Ukraine: Changing Course towards a European Future.*

Washington, DC: Center for Transatlantic Relations, 2011.

Center for Transatlantic Relations
The Paul H. Nitze School of Advanced International Studies
The Johns Hopkins University
1717 Massachusetts Ave., NW, Suite 525
Washington, DC 20036
Tel: (202) 663-5880
Fax (202) 663-5879
Email: transatlantic@jhu.edu
http://transatlantic.sais-jhu.edu

ISBN 0-9848544-2-8
ISBN 978-0-9848544-2-4

Cover photo credits, clockwise from upper left: Sergey Kamshylin/Fotolia.com, Michal Bednarek/123rf.com, frog-travel/Fololia.com, Gudellaphoto/Fotolia.com, Vladimir Nikulin/123rf.com

Table of Contents

Preface and Acknowledgements

Events in Ukraine are headline issues and there is considerable uncertainty about the direction of the country. With this in mind, the SAIS Center for Transatlantic Relations at Johns Hopkins University and Poland's Institute for Eastern Studies, the organizer of the annual Economic Forum in Krynica, Poland, asked the authors in this volume to address current issues related to Ukraine's domestic and international situation, and to recommend steps that could be taken to forge a more democratic, prosperous and secure Ukraine. Our intention is to evoke the political, economic and foreign policy possibilities of an open Ukraine in the heart of Europe.

This project succeeded because of the partnership between our two institutions. On behalf of the authors we would like to thank the many colleagues who participated in the deliberations and meetings that produced this book, including participants in the Ukraine Policy Forum, our Center's regular meeting series examining Ukraine's current challenges and future possibilities.

We would also like to thank our colleagues at the Center for Transatlantic Relations and the Institute for Eastern Studies for their help and good cheer throughout this project, and Peggy Irvine and Peter Lindeman for working with us on the many details related to the production of the book. We are grateful to the Austrian Marshall Plan Foundation, which supports our work on Central European issues.

Our authors express their own views, and do not necessarily reflect views of any institution or government.

Taras Kuzio
Daniel Hamilton

Towards an Open Ukraine:
Policy Recommendations

Ukraine is one of the biggest, but also the second poorest country in Europe after Moldova. Given its territorial size, its geographic position, its almost 50 million population and its role as the main transit state for Russian oil and gas exports to central and western Europe, Ukraine has been a critical strategic factor for Euro-Atlantic and Eurasian security in the two decades of its independence. Today, it stands at a critical crossroads between developing a more open society increasingly integrated into the European space of democracy, prosperity and market-based economics grounded in respect for human rights and the rule of law, or an increasingly autocratic system, mired in the economic stagnation and political instability that is historically characteristic of Europe's borderlands. The choice is straightforward: Ukraine can either join the European mainstream or remain in a gray zone of insecurity between Europe and Russia.

The following recommendations outline how Ukraine could move away from immobility in the gray zone of domestic and international politics in which it finds itself, break its reform logjam and become an Open Ukraine—a democracy accountable to its people with a socially responsible market economy, governed by an administration that respects the rule of law, fights corruption and that can effectively implement needed reforms, and that is increasingly integrated into the European mainstream. These proposals are intended to expand the horizons of Ukrainian elites and opinion leaders and equip them with concrete reasons to move from short-term "momentocracy" to a more powerful vision that could guide their country. They also suggest ways Ukraine's neighbors can make the costs and benefits of Ukraine's choices clear.

Political Reforms and Democratization

Ukraine's fundamental problem has been government dysfunction with leaders changing the constitution and election laws to deny power to the opposition or maximize power for themselves after elections. For Ukraine to have more effective governance, it must tackle seven interrelated challenges: switching from a presidential to a parliamentary political system, which is better suited for encouraging democratization; parliamentary and legislative reform; administrative reform; strengthening the rule of law; judicial reform; eradicating systemic corruption; and strengthening civil society and independent media.

- *Switch to a Parliamentary System.* The scholarly and policy debate has been extensive whether presidentialism or parliamentrism is best suited for countries in transition. Of the 27 post-communist states, those with successful democracies in Central-Eastern Europe have adopted parliamentary systems while authoritarian regimes in Eurasia are primarily built on presidential systems. Parliamentary systems have therefore been successful in promoting democracy and European integration than presidential systems. Ukraine has had a presidential system for a decade (1996-2005) and again since 2010 when the Constitutional Court ruled under pressure from the executive that constitutional reforms adopted in December 2004 and going into effect after the March 2006 elections were 'unconstitutional' (the same Court had refused to consider the same question under President Viktor Yushchenko). Presidentialism in Ukraine has stifled democratic developments, encouraged authoritarianism, promoted censorship of the media and became a nexus of corruption and illegality. Unelected regional governors, which duplicate elected local councils and mayors, have traditionally been at the center of election fraud, patronage and corruption. Abuses of presidentialism are clearly evident under President Viktor Yanukovych, who has sought to maximize power at the expense of parliament, the Cabinet, regions and local councils.

- *Parliamentary and Legislative Reform.* A strong and independent legislature is vital for jump-starting the reform process in Ukraine, yet the Ukrainian parliament turned into a rubber-stamp body with minimal political authority. Open Ukraine requires legislation, drafted in a transparent manner and be open to public deliberation, that would ensure a level playing field for competing political parties and their fair representation in the parliament. The mixed system, adopted in November 2011 ignoring recommendations by the Council of Europe's Venice Commission, prevents this by skewing election results in favor of the Party of Regions. Provisions for full disclosure of candidates' funding sources and for challenging election results are essential for a democracy. The law should limit the ability of electoral commissions to interfere with the electoral process. The parliament's role in choosing candidates for Cabinet positions must be revived. It must also have strong oversight powers over the executive. Internal rules for coalition formation should prioritize party factions over individual deputies; the majority coalition should be formed based solely on parties elected to the parliament and not, as has been the tradition until now, of new parties and factions created after elections within the life of parliaments. There should also be a strict enforcement of the rules requiring deputies to vote individually (that is, a halt to the widespread practice of absentee voting) and disclose their personal incomes. The legislative process should be streamlined to improve the quality of legislation, possibly with the assistance of a Council of Foreign Advisers, as was the case in the first half of the 1990s.

- *Administrative Reform.* The executive needs to be streamlined and decentralized to allow for more effective and accurate application of law. Many government ministries and state committees have overlapping responsibilities, duplicating functions and wasting resources.

- *Strengthen the Rule of Law.* In Ukraine the law continues to be viewed as an instrument of partisan governmental power. That which is construed to be "illegal" is whatever the government in power finds to be politically expedient. Procedural safeguards that are at the heart of a rule of law legal system are absent or ignored. Ukraine should fundamentally and profoundly transform its legal system if it is to spread European values and the rule of law. This means coming to grips with the legal system's catastrophic Soviet past; reforming the legal academy; and reforming the laws, procedures and mechanisms that remain in place as holdovers from Ukraine's totalitarian legacy. The Prosecutor's office needs to be overhauled or replaced. It has become highly compromised through corruption and under Yanukovych it has returned to its Soviet function as a state arm of repression.

- *Judicial Reform.* In a system that respects the rule of law, judges are professional, independent and impartial; they are not "accountable" to prosecutors. Prosecutors, in turn, do not act as the partisan political arm of the government. That is not the case in Ukraine today. The court system is endemically corrupt, incompetent and subject to commercial and political influence. Judges are routinely bribed to secure convictions or release of those charged or to alter title deeds in businesses in the widespread practice of corporate raiding. The President exerts political influence over the judiciary through the High Council of Justice, which is dominated by representatives of the ruling party and the Chairman of the Security Service, a direct conflict of interest. Ukraine's judicial system is in dire need of overhaul. The competence and jurisdiction of differing courts must be clarified. Training and selection of judges need to be made more transparent and meritocratic. Courts and judges require sufficient financing so as to discourage corruption. Concepts along these lines were approved five years ago, but have yet to be implemented. Court proceedings should be made more transparent, impartial, and effective. Procedures for mediation, independent arbitration, and enhanced use of notaries should be introduced. The power of the High Council of Justice to select or discipline judges should be transferred to a non-partisan body comprising of authoritative and experienced judges, such as the High Qualifications Commission. The President's and Parliament's role in appointing or removing judges should be limited to mere approval of the Commission's recommendations with few clearly specified exceptions.

- *Eradicate Systemic Corruption.* The presence or absence of rule of law in a society is closely related to the level of corruption. Corruption has become endemic in Ukraine and is growing; it has degraded the country's governance, undermined its democracy, reduced public trust in state institutions, distorted the economy, discouraged foreign direct investment and been exported to Europe. To reduce corruption, Ukraine needs political leadership committed to and greater societal awareness that corruption impedes economic development, democratization and European integration. Organizations and individuals committed to combating corruption need to mobilize behind specific, concrete initiatives—such as draft laws regarding codes of criminal procedure, professional ethics, and financial declarations by public servants. There is a wealth of international experience on how to reduce corruption, particularly from other post-Soviet or post-socialist countries; Ukraine should take advantage of such experience.

• ***Strengthen Civil Society and Independent Media.*** Media censorship under Yanukovych has not yet reached the level characteristic of Kuchma's presidency and is different in nature. Nonetheless, even though major media outlets in Ukraine have not yet fallen fully under the government's control, their independence has eroded substantially due to the excessive interference of owners keen to remain on good terms with the executive in news coverage. Television news is dominated by good media coverage of the authorities and either paints the opposition in a negative light or ignores them. Only print and internet-based media still function as an instrument of accountability and a source of reliable news. Further international assistance to these media outlets is vital for supporting media pluralism.

Economic Growth and Modernization

During the last two decades Ukraine has moved from a command administrative system but has still to arrive at the final destination of a market economy, despite recognition by the U.S. and EU in 2005-2006 of a 'market economy' status. Ukraine's 'partial reform equilibrium' is stuck between the Soviet past and European future and only concerted reforms will move the economy towards a European-style social market economy. Ukraine was hit hard by the global economic and financial crisis. The combination of weaker demand from Ukraine's trading partners, falling export prices, rising import prices and reduced access to international financial markets sliced GDP by 14.8% in 2009, and it will take until 2013 to recover that lost ground. Inflation is hovering above 9% and unemployment at 8%. The *hryvnia*, Ukraine's national currency, has lost almost half of its value against the U.S. dollar since July 2008. Pension expenditures increased from 9% of GDP in 2003 to 17.6% in 2010, one of the highest levels in the world—yet pension fund revenues cover only two-thirds of expenditures, the rest being covered by transfers from the budget. Demographic pressures will increase the burden on the working population even further. Ukraine's successful accession to the WTO in May 2008, after 15 years of negotiations, was an isolated foreign policy achievement of the Yushchenko presidency. President Yanukovych launched reforms in summer 2010, but implementation has been very slow due to a lack of political will, populist concessions ahead of parliamentary elections in 2012, and a deficit in government capacity to draft EU-compatible legislation. The refusal to implement further stages of the 2010 MF agreement, including raising household utility prices for a second time, has led to the suspension of IMF tranches. It is imperative that Ukraine return to the IMF agreement in order to introduce reforms and boost foreign investor confidence.

The following areas are urgent on the road to an Open Ukraine:

- *Pension reform* has been long delayed, yet is critically important for restoring Ukraine's financial sustainability. The IMF demand to raise the pension age from 55 to 60, as part of the July 2010 agreement for Ukraine, was adopted by parliament in 2011.

- *Simplified taxation and licensing,* including simplified accounting of revenues, should be introduced for small and medium businesses. Previously introduced reform principles must be made operational, such as the "one-stop shop" for registering and licensing businesses. Any permits other than those directly stipulated by the law should be abolished. Remaining permits and activities subject to mandatory licensing should be compiled into a single piece of legislation.

- *Corporate legislation reform.* The Economic Code of Ukraine is a confused mix of Soviet command economy elements and market institutions. It should be abandoned. The Civil Code of Ukraine should comply with EU Directives on company law. The new law on joint stock companies must be amended to comply with EU Directives on company law, and internationally accepted principles of corporate law and corporate governance best practices, by replacing the profit-extracting legal model for such companies to one of investor protection. Modern legal structures are needed for small and medium enterprises and domestic and foreign investors via a separate limited liability company law that provides for an efficient system of governance, control bodies and reliable protection of minority participants. The law on re-establishing solvency of a debtor or declaring a debtor bankrupt must be amended to prevent abuses by related-party (conflict of interest) transactions and by enhancing the personal responsibility (liability) of company officers and the bankruptcy commissioner.

- *Agricultural Reform.* The moratorium on trading agricultural land should be ended and free access of citizens and agricultural producers to land resources ensured. Prices for agricultural land should be liberalized and work on establishing a land cadastre should be continued. Consideration should be given to allowing foreigners and foreign-owned companies to own some agricultural land deposits (e.g. up to 10% of land in each region *[oblast]*). Such reforms would attract more capital, help to import and disseminate modern agricultural technologies, and facilitate greater access to international channels of distribution of agricultural products. Moreover, Ukraine has a strong interest in the liberalization of global trade in foodstuffs. Administrative restrictions on exports should be abandoned and delays in VAT refunds to exporters urgently fixed. Targeted income support measures should be introduced for poor families to compensate for the rise in foodstuff prices. Social support and re-training programs for redundant agricultural workers need strengthening. Ukrainian law on state support of agriculture should be consolidated into one piece of legislation. An information service for agricultural markets should be established to monitor and forecast global food markets and collect information on standards in other countries. Sanitary and safety standards should, as a matter of high priority, be aligned with international and EU norms. Establishing WTO-compatible free trade agreements with other non-EU trade partners is in Ukrainian interests.

Energy Efficiency and Independence

Ukraine's energy sector is plagued by aging infrastructure, widespread corruption, political manipulation of utility rates and statistics, and minimal foreign direct investment. Although Ukraine has oil, gas and coal reserves, it is one of the most energy inefficient economies in the world and only able to cover 47-49% of its energy demand. Gas imports account for 7-8% of Ukrainian GDP and are clearly unsustainable. Around half of Ukraine's total energy consumption comes from natural gas. Although Ukraine has large conventional and unconventional gas resources, it will be unable to boost domestic gas production without deeper and comprehensive reforms and significant foreign direct investment. While it has coal reserves for another 100 years, the productivity of coal extraction is very low and its production costs are high. Coal mining is highly dangerous and Ukraine has one of the highest rates of accidents in the world, close to Chinese levels. Without restructuring, modernization and liberalized market reforms, Ukraine will be unable to cope with its energy supply challenges, including decreasing its extremely high energy consumption.

Moreover, Ukraine is deeply dependent on Russia, which supplies 85-90% of Ukraine's oil imports and 75-80% of its natural gas imports. In addition, in 2010 Ukraine signed agreements with Russia to build two nuclear reactors and to deliver only Russian fuel to all Ukrainian reactors until they cease operation. These arrangements have stunted necessary domestic reforms and weakened Ukraine's bargaining position vis-à-vis Russia, particularly with regard to gas imports and transit. Moscow uses the gas issue to exert pressure on Kyiv over various bilateral issues. Kyiv signed a gas agreement with Moscow disadvantageous to Ukrainian interests, yet Moscow insists that any review of that agreement would only be possible if the state gas company *Naftohaz Ukrainy* merged with *Gazprom*, ownership of the Ukrainian GTS was transferred to *Gazprom*, or if Ukraine joined Russia's Customs Union with Belarus and Kazakhstan. Yanukovych has publicly rejected such conditions as "humiliating," and Ukrainian law prevents the selling, renting or leasing of critical energy infrastructures to foreign countries and companies. Russia is pushing for a new gas consortium over the GTS acquiring majority control, leaving Ukraine just 20% of its shares. Such an arrangement would question Ukrainian sovereignty and independence, threaten efforts at deeper democratic and market reforms, and pose considerable challenges to EU energy security and foreign policy. Giving up sovereignty over the GTS is seen by the Nikolai Azarov government as a better option than implementing unpopular IMF reforms (such as raising household uility prices to reduce Naftohaz Ukrainy's contribution of 2% to the budget deficit) as Russia will provide gas at a subsidized price in a new contract.

An Open Ukraine requires Kyiv to boost domestic energy efficiency; eradicate endemic corruption in the energy sector; adopt all of the elements in the European Energy Community that it signed on to; and diversify its energy mix and strengthen its national security by reducing its dependence on Russia.

- *Boosting Energy Efficiency.* Ukraine's energy infrastructure is inefficient and wasteful. The country has invested little in energy efficiency, yet such efforts are critical to Ukraine's energy security. A major step forward would be for Kyiv to take the politically unpopular decision to raise gas prices for households and utilities, which are heavily subsidized (a first increase was undertaken in 2010 but the Cabinet balked at taking a second increase ahead of the 2012 elections). The domestic political fallout could be mitigated by compensatory measures for low income households. Artificially low gas prices in the past have dampened any incentive to boost domestic gas extraction or to improve efficiency and a new gas contract with a return to subsidized prices will again freeze Ukraine's inefficient and wasteful energy sector. These have fuelled high-price gas imports from Russia, compromising

Ukraine's national energy security and its overall economic competitiveness. Most Ukrainian energy producers have been unable to finance even their replacement investments because their revenues from domestic sales do not cover their costs. The only real beneficiary of the artificially increased demand for gas is the Russian state gas company Gazprom. In contrast, the Ukrainian state gas company Naftohaz Ukrainy needs budgetary support because of highly subsidized utility prices.

- *Eliminate endemic corruption in the energy sector.* The lack of strong market reforms is linked to systemic corruption and a nebulous legal and legislative framework, which have unnerved the markets and scared away foreign investment. If Ukraine is serious about its energy security, it will work to eradicate systemic corruption and establish clear legal ground rules for investments in its energy sector.

- *Adopt European Standards.* On February 1, 2011 Ukraine became a full member of the European Energy Community (EEC), which extends the EU's internal energy market to Ukraine. It is strongly in Kyiv's interest to live up to the obligations such membership entails, including full adherence to anti-corruption norms of European law and implementation of the EU's third energy package of unbundling energy production from its distribution in gas and electricity markets by January 2015. The implications of this third package are far-reaching and often not fully understood. EEC members are obliged not only to revise their laws and to adopt secondary legislation but also to promote fundamental changes in market structures by introducing market rules and legislation. Central European practice offers Ukraine a means to implement EU *acquis* in energy despite its dense interwoven ties with Russia, whereby long-term Russian contracts could enjoy temporary derogation from EU regulations.

- *Diversify.* Energy cooperation with the EU and other foreign partners could help Kyiv diversify its fossil-fuel imports and its overall energy mix and reduce its dependence on Russian gas and oil. Ukraine has excellent wind resources and possesses significant unconventional (shale) gas deposits.

Ukraine's Parliament has already passed more investor-friendly legislation to open its domestic natural gas market to foreign shale gas and coal-bed producers. Exploitation of these reserves could give buyers more leverage to renegotiate the high Russian oil-indexed gas price demands that are included in long-term contracts, and could drastically reduce Ukrainian dependence on Russian gas. Moreover, the confluence of EU energy market liberalization, stepped-up antitrust enforcement, and the emergence of unconventional gas supplies in European markets may prompt Russia to increase its own efforts at energy efficiency and to invest in its own unconventional gas resources, which may be much cheaper than investing in the extremely costly Yamal Peninsula and Shtokman projects, and perhaps lead to greater reciprocity and symmetry in both Ukrainian and EU energy relations with Russia. On the other hand, if Ukrainian and European gas policies remain hostage to long-term contracts, "take-and-pay" clauses and oil price linkages, prospects will be dim for new and sustainable integrated energy and climate policies, despite the fact that international gas markets have de-linked from oil price markets.

A Strategy for the West:
Open Door, Straight Talk, Tough Love

Given Kyiv's turn to autocracy, it would be tempting for Western policymakers, besieged with other priorities, to turn their backs on Ukraine. This would be a strategic mistake. The United States and the EU have a strong stake in an Open Ukraine secure in its borders and politically stable. A more autocratic, isolated and divided Ukraine would be a source of continued instability in the heart of Europe. It would make it harder for Georgia and Moldova to pursue their pro-Western course. It would diminish prospects for reform in Belarus. It would perpetuate a gray zone of borderlands on a continent that has until now enjoyed an historically rare moment to transcend the tragedies of its past divisions. Western leaders should avoid falling into the same short-term mindset that currently befalls Ukrainian elites, and adopt a broader strategic perspective.

Ukraine is beset by regional and cultural divisions that will have a profound impact on the country's political evolution. As Ukrainians debate the norms that should guide their society, normative consistency by their Western partners can provide orientation and strength. This does not mean softening norms or conditions for effective engagement, but it does mean being clear about the benefits that could result from adherence to such norms. The West has a vested interest in ensuring that Ukrainian leaders understand the opportunities and consequences that could result from their decisions, and should be consistent in setting forth a coherent and coordinated framework of relations that can help shape those choices.

As Ukraine struggles to find its place in 21st century Europe, therefore, the door to that Europe should be kept open. There is no consensus at present within the EU about the possibility of ultimate Ukrainian membership. Yet if the door to Europe is closed, the Ukrainian government will have little incentive to advance political and economic reforms, and could either turn to alternative geopolitical frameworks or remain isolated in a geopolitical gray zone, generating instability and insecurity throughout its wider neighborhood. Clear EU support for the principle of the Open Door, on the other hand, can help Ukrainians build the courage and political will to implement tough reforms at home—not as a favor to others, but because they understand it is in their own interest to do so. have an effect on internal developments in Ukraine. And if Kyiv begins to implement reforms that promise to move Ukraine towards an open, democratic and market-based society, such actions can in turn affect what leaders in EU capitals are willing to offer Ukraine.

Based on the continued validity of the Open Door, Western strategy should advance along two tracks that work together. The first track should demonstrate the genuine interest of North America and Europe in close and cooperative ties with Ukraine, and should set forth in concrete terms the potential benefits of more productive relations. They should make it very clear that Europe and the U.S. stand as willing partners if Ukraine decides to invest in its people, forge effective democratic institutions, build a more sustainable economy grounded in the rule of law, tackle endemic corruption, diversify and reform its energy economy; and build better relations with its neighbors. U.S. and European efforts should seek to strengthen democratic institutions; promote the growth of civil society, especially independent media; support economic reforms; provide technical assistance for energy reforms; and facilitate interaction between Ukrainian citizens and their neighbors, including visa liberalization, business and student exchanges. If Kyiv signals by its actions that it is interested in deepening its engagement with the West, North America and the EU should be equally ready to engage while pushing for more comprehensive economic and political reforms aimed at facilitating Ukraine's integration into Euro-Atlantic institutions.

At the same time the U.S. and Europe should make it clear that if Ukraine's leadership abuses the rule of law, facilitates corruption, fails to advance effective reforms, and resorts to intimidation tactics, as is currently the case regarding the Tymoshenko conviction, the prospects for an open, prosperous and secure European Ukraine will fade. International efforts to deter Ukraine's further backsliding should combine the threat of costly sanctions towards the ruling elite with calls for unencumbered engagement of citizens in political life, targeted assistance to key civil society actors and specific proposals for reforms that could pave the way toward a more open Ukraine. Outside pressure on Ukrainian authorities clearly has its limits, of course, and the main brunt of responsibility for the evolution of Ukraine's political regime lies with domestic actors. However, as the Orange Revolution demonstrated, Western influence can restrict the range of options available to authorities who choose to fight their own people, and can help to weaken the internal legitimacy of some of the government's anti-democratic policies.

In short, a proactive Western policy might be best characterized as Open Door, Straight Talk, and Tough Love. Such an approach requires persistence, patience, and consistent engagement on the following priorities:

- *Support Civil Society.* By monopolizing political space and marginalizing the opposition, Ukrainian authorities undermine the reform process and weaken public trust in government activities. Transformative reforms of the magnitude needed in Ukraine require support across the country and from political forces on both sides of the major political divide. North American and European governments and international organizations should stress the critical importance of a free and fair parliamentary campaign in October 2012 ahead of the process and cast a spotlight on even minor violations of democratic procedures. They should weigh in against any signs of abuse of state-administrative resources or biased limitations on opposition activity or campaign financing, in order to prevent further emasculation of civic groups or further closure of the civic space for independent political action. They should encourage Kyiv to lower barriers to independent media and to ensure media access to the opposition. They should encourage active involvement of opposition parties and leading NGOs in the process of drafting reform strategies and ensuring government accountability at all levels. International organizations should provide technical assistance in training election observers and electoral commission members representing all political parties.

- *Advocate Institutional Reform.* Western governments and international organizations, particularly representatives of post-communist countries, should advocate targeted institutional reforms aimed at establishing a legally-grounded balance of authority among the executive, legislative and judicial branches; increasing the government's accountability to the parliament; and strengthening oversight agencies, such as an independent anticorruption bureau, accounting chamber, the office of the ombudsman and the financial regulatory body. They should offer concrete suggestions to depoliticize the judiciary and the civil service, which are still dominated by vested political and business interests.

- *Support Ukrainian Efforts to Tackle Systemic Corruption.* The West should develop consistent medium- to long-term strategies to help Ukraine fundamentally reform its legal system and to reduce systemic corruption.

- *Offer Technical Support for Reforms.* Ukraine's Cabinet lacks staff to develop draft legislation and government employees are not qualified enough to develop modern economic legislation. Provision of technical assistance will be crucial to

Ukrainian political, administrative, economic and energy reforms.

- ***Be Clear about the Consequences of Undemocratic Activities.*** North America and the EU demonstrated impressive unanimity in condemning the trial and conviction of Yulia Tymoshenko in October 2011 and issued strong demands for her release and resumption of her ability to participate in the political life of the country. They should link such condemnation with concrete measures that would raise the cost to Ukrainian authorities of further undemocratic steps. Such measures should include suspension of Ukraine's membership in the Council of Europe; introducing visa bans for those officials responsible for ordering the crackdown against protesters or persecution of the opposition; a freeze on negotiations for an Association Agreement (including the DCFTA); and limiting bilateral contacts with top Ukrainian officials and state visits to Kyiv. At the same time, the West must maintain its clear message that the door to Europe and Euro-Atlantic institutions remains open should Ukraine work to create the conditions by which it could in fact walk through that door.

- ***Make Better Use of the Eastern Partnership.*** In order to articulate a policy for neighbors for whom membership is a distant goal, the EU launched the Eastern Partnership in 2009 with Armenia, Azerbaijan, Belarus, Georgia, Moldova, and Ukraine. Yet instead of using the EaP to deepen engagement in Ukraine and other Partnership countries, EU officials dampen their own influence with rhetoric that distances themselves from the prospect of a space of stability, prosperity and democracy stretching as far across the European continent as possible. The EU should be far more proactive in its use of the Eastern Partnership.

  - *Combine Broad Visa Liberalization with Targeted Restrictions.* Kyiv has a strong interest in visa liberalization with the EU; one in every ten Schengen visas goes to a Ukrainian. The EU should calibrate its approach by offering a generous broad-based approach to visa liberalization for Ukrainian citizens (particularly young people and students) and facilitating special possibilities for study abroad and cultural, educational, business and local government exchanges, so that the average man and woman in the street, especially in the east and south of the country, can gain personal awareness of the benefits to be derived from closer relations. This strategy of maintaining an Open Europe for Ukrainian citizens should be combined with targeted visa bans and restrictions for Ukrainian officials engaged in undemocratic or illegal activities.

- *Engage Ukraine Actively via a Transcarpathian Macro-Regional Strategy.* New EU macro-regional strategies, for instance with the Danube states, offer a potential model for engagement with Carpathian states. This special area is surrounded by four EU member states, namely Poland, Slovakia, Hungary and Romania. All four are neighbors to Transcarpathia and to each other by cultural, historical and ethnic ties. The Transcarpathian Region could be developed into a strategic Ukrainian bridgehead for integration into Europe. It is already linked by broad-gauge railway to Hungary and Slovakia, and its special location and multiethnic traditions are convenient for offshore zones and assembling factories.

- *Support Ukraine's Democratic Development.* The proposed European Endowment for Democracy should disburse aid to Ukrainian civil society and encourage and defend Ukraine's democratic development to monitor Eastern Partnership policy toward Ukraine. The EU should ensure that its assistance is coordinated with U.S. and Canadian efforts to ensure they are complementary and not duplicative.

- **Use the Association Agreement and DCFTA to Advance the Broader Strategy.** With neither NATO nor EU membership on the horizon, the primary vehicle for keeping open the prospect for Ukraine's closer ties to the European mainstream is the Association Agreement and Deep Comprehensive Free Trade Agreement (DCFTA) currently being negotiated between Ukraine and the EU. However, the EU has frozen the final negotiations slated to led to initialing of the agreement, due to concerns in various EU member states about the political repression and serious violations of rule of law—particularly the arrest and trial of former prime minister Tymoshenko—that have occurred since President Yanukovych took office. The DCFTA offers the EU a mechanism by which it can calibrate a two-track approach to Ukraine. Initialing the agreement would signal that the EU is indeed ready to move forward with a much closer relationship with Ukraine, with concrete and substantial benefits for the Ukrainian government, Ukrainian elites, and Ukrainian citizens. But freezing the formal signing and ratification process would also signal that a fundamentally new partnership is only possible on the basis of respect for human rights and the rule of law.

The DCFTA is in fact a new generation economic agreement ranging far beyond a standard free trade agreement, not only liberalizing 95% of bilateral trade but aiming for deep and comprehensive harmonization of economic legislation. The opportunities for Ukraine are immense, given that the EU is the largest single market in the world, about 130 times larger than the Ukrainian domestic market and 15-20 times larger than the Russian, Belarus and Kazakhstan markets combined. The benefits to all sectors of Ukrainian society of joining the DCFTA far outweigh the small number of benefits from entering a free trade agreement with the CIS.

- *Keep NATO's Open Door while Engaging Closely.* Ukrainian membership in NATO has again been pushed off the international agenda for the immediate future. While the door to NATO membership remains open to Ukraine (and Georgia) in principle, in reality there is little support in Western capitals for further enlargement of the Alliance in the near term. Focusing on NATO membership now will only inflame the political atmosphere and make progress in other important areas more difficult. The main obstacle is not Russian opposition—though this is an important factor—but low public support for membership in Ukraine itself.[1] On the other

---

[1] Popular support for NATO—22-25 percent and below 10 percent in the Russified areas of eastern Ukraine—is much lower in Ukraine in comparison to other states in Eastern Europe. See the chapter by F. Stephen Larrabee.

hand, Ukraine was the first CIS state to join the Partnership for Peace, has been one of the most active participants in its exercises, and the NATO-Ukraine Charter on a Distinctive Partnership gives Ukraine a unique status. Rapprochement with NATO increased Ukraine's freedom of maneuver and led to an improvement of ties with Moscow. Ukraine contributes to nearly all UN and NATO peacekeeping operations, in some cases more than some NATO members.

Nonetheless, as long as only about a quarter of the population favors membership, prospects for Ukraine being admitted to NATO remain remote. In the meantime, other steps in the security field could be taken to strengthen cooperation within the NATO-Ukraine Partnership in areas where there is mutual interest, while encouraging progress toward more open democratic institutions. Such activities include engaging the Ukrainian military in a dialogue on military reform; continuing to involve Ukraine in peacekeeping operations, both within NATO and bilaterally; enhancing cooperation on nuclear safety; further developing the crisis consultative mechanism; and further developing ties in such areas as civil-military relations, democratic control of the armed forces, armaments cooperation, and defense planning. Information campaigns should highlight how NATO provides practical help to Ukraine in emergency situations, cyber-security, security to the Euro-2012 soccer championship, orders for Ukrainian industry, and support for the training of Ukrainian officers. A critical area of concern, as Ukraine turns autocratic, is democratic control and reform of internal security forces (Security Service, Interior Ministry, border guards, customs officers, Prosecutor's office), which are far larger than the armed forces, and which are used in political repression and involved in corruption.

- ***Engage Ukraine on Its Own Merits, Not as a Subset of Russia Policy***. A successful Euro-Atlantic policy of engagement toward Ukraine cannot be a subset of Western policy toward Russia; the West must consider its own substantial interests in an open Ukraine on their own merits. At the same time, the

United States, Canada and European allies should send a clear message to Moscow that they oppose any attempts to undermine the sovereignty of Russia's neighbors, including threats to their territorial integrity. Upon entering office Yanukovych acted quickly to remove key irritants with Moscow, such as the international campaign to recognize the *Holdomor* (1933 artificial famine) was genocide; shelving plans to join NATO; and ramming through an unconstitutional measure that prolongs the stationing of the Russian Black Sea Fleet in Crimea to 2042-2047. Russia has demanded more, however, including Ukrainian membership in its CIS Customs Union or Russian ownership of the Ukrainian GTS. It is clear that Russia finds it very hard to respect Ukrainian sovereignty and independence. Yanukovych has received little in return for his efforts at appeasing Moscow, and despite his interest in closer relations with Russia, he has also shown that he still prefers being the leader of a sovereign country to being the governor of a Russian province. Nonetheless, he faces strong and consistent Russian pressure on key issues; Western policy should make the implications of his choices clear. For instance, Ukraine faces a choice between entering the CIS Customs Union of Russia, Belarus and Kazakhstan, which is likely to block all fundamental domestic market reforms; or proceeding with the kinds of domestic reforms that would enable Ukraine to reap the benefits of the DCFTA with the EU and closer integration with the European mainstream, including visa liberalization, competitiveness, transparency and accountability in Ukraine's energy markets, greater investments in infrastructure and new technologies, and reduced energy dependency. The first choice demands far less than the second choice in terms of domestic reform, but the second choice promises substantially greater rewards. And joining the Eurasian Customs Union with countries that are not members of the WTO (Russia may soon join, but not Belarus and Kazakhstan) would require a renegotiation of Ukraine's membership in the WTO and end Ukraine's hopes for an Association Agreement and DCFTA.

We have no illusions about the difficulty of realizing the vision of an Open Ukraine. Yet the gains, both for Ukraine and for Europe, would be considerable. Ukraine's choices are its to make, but it is the West's responsibility to make the costs and benefits of those choices clear and credible to Ukraine's leaders and its citizens.

Introduction:
Why an Open Ukraine is the Best Path for its Citizens, its Elites, and its Neighbors

Taras Kuzio and Daniel Hamilton

In this volume a number of distinguished experts offer analysis and recommendations in politics, the economy, rule of law and corruption, national identity, energy, European integration and foreign policy. Together these contributions set forth a vision for an Open Ukraine, a democracy accountable to its people with a socially responsible market economy, governed by an administration that respects the rule of law, fights corruption and that can effectively implement needed reforms, and that is increasingly integrated into the European mainstream. This vision of Open Ukraine would fulfill the country's enormous potential, which has been beyond the grasp of every Ukrainian administration since independence.

Major strides forward in democratization following the 2004 Orange Revolution were combined with political instability and economic growth, until the 2008 global financial crisis. The Freedom House human rights think tank upgraded Ukraine to 'Free,' the only country in the CIS to receive this ranking. Progress in democratization in some areas, notably democratic elections and free media, however, were not matched by progress in the rule of law, fighting corruption and democratic control of law enforcement structures. Bohdan Vitvitsky and Stephen Larrabee discuss how the failure to combat these factors led to public disillusionment in the leaders of the Orange Revolution and made it relatively easy to quickly dismantle Ukraine's democratic gains following Viktor Yanukovych's narrow 3% election victory in February 2010.

Widespread U.S., Canadian and European hopes that President Yanukovych had accepted the democratic rules of the game and was therefore different from Prime Minister Yanukovych, who had been accused of having orchestrated election fraud seven years earlier, have proven to be unfounded. Today, a concerted effort is under way to build an autocratic regime, with significant implications for Ukrainian society and Ukraine's integration into Europe, again preventing the country from fulfilling its potential as an Open Ukraine. In this regard, the conviction of former Prime Minister and opposition leader Yulia Tymoshenko in October 2011 to seven years imprisonment and three years ban from holding office is a watershed event, the most visible and emblematic manifestation of the country's turn away from Europe toward autocracy. The sentence has jeopardized Ukraine's chances of entering into an Association Agreement (including a Deep and Comprehensive Free Trade Agreement—DCFTA) with the EU that has been under negotiation since 2008, when the country joined the WTO. Integration into Europe, while not the full membership that a majority of Ukrainians support, would bring enormous benefits of access to the world's largest trading area, giving unlimited opportunities for the Ukrainian economy and its companies; institutional and legislative alignment that would strengthen the country's state-building processes; and visa-free access for citizens—all areas analyzed in great detail by Peter Balazs in his chapter in this volume. If Ukraine's leaders truly desire an Open Ukraine, then European integration is the country's best—and only—option.

Ukraine held four democratic elections between December 2004 and February 2010, but concern whether future elections would remain democratic became evident in widespread European and U.S. criticism of the conduct of October 2010 local elections, which failed to meet international standards. With Tymoshenko and other opposition leaders in jail it will be difficult for the OSCE and Council of Europe to recognize the 2012 elections as democratic. The conduct of parliamentary elections in October 2012 and strategic decisions about much-needed reforms will remain key benchmarks for Ukraine's likely direction over the coming decade. Other manifestations of democratic backsliding since 2010 include a decline in media freedom and the right to peaceful assembly, the erosion of parliamentary independence and monopolization of political power, and un-democratic practices against the opposition by the Interior Ministry, Prosecutor-General's office and Security Service (SBU).

While the crucial domestic and foreign policy decisions are for Ukrainians to take, signals sent from abroad could make a difference. The policy recommendations and expert opinions outlined in this volume present an alternative direction to that taking place in Ukraine, a path that is beneficial to all sectors of society and all regions of Ukraine, a path towards an Open Ukraine.

Despite the country's great potential, its political culture has been a "momentocracy," a Yushchenko reference to a collection of short-term policies that benefit a small group of elite insiders yet lack longer-term vision or strategies towards a better future for the country as a whole. A number of factors, most of which tend to feed on each other, have rendered Ukraine an immobile state[1] that exists not for its citizens but instead for the benefit of a small group of ruling elites, who remain concerned only with dividing up a rather small existing pie, rather than expanding that pie through reforms that could lift the lives of its people and integrate the country into a much larger space of prosperity, democracy and security. As Frank Umbach points out, the most brazen example of the prioritization of short term rents at the expense of reforms is the country's unreformed energy sector. With very few exceptions, Ukrainian politicians have succumbed to the temptation of seeing the energy sector as a cash cow for short term financial gain.[2]

The first factor inhibiting Ukraine from moving beyond an immobile state is the Soviet legacy of state control: deeply embedded traditions of markets distorted by monopolies, systemic corruption, manipulated elections, and a politically captive judiciary. When the Soviet Union disintegrated, Ukraine had to undertake a "quadruple transition." It needed to create the mechanisms and institutions of a sovereign state; build a nation from a quasi-republic in the Soviet empire; transform the command-administrative Soviet economy into a market economy; and establish an effective democracy out of a totalitarian

---

[1] This phrase is taken from Taras Kuzio, "Political Culture and Democracy: Ukraine as an Immobile State," *East European Politics and Society*, vol. 25, no. 1 (February 2011), pp. 88–113.

[2] This was pointed out in detail by Margarita Balmaceda in *Energy Dependency, Politics and Corruption in the Former Soviet Union: Russia's Power, Oligarch's Profits and Ukraine's Missing Energy Policy, 1995–2006* (London and New York: Routledge, 2008).

political system. Ukraine has been only partly successful, and since 2010 some critical gains have been reversed, as Serhiy Kudelia succinctly analyses in his chapter on the politics of the Yushchenko and Yanukovych presidencies.

A second factor important to Ukraine is national integration. Ukrainian society is divided along regional lines, and between Russian and Ukrainian language speakers, which makes it more difficult to consolidate Ukraine's elites around united goals of democratic and market economic reforms, improving the rule of law, reducing corruption and clear foreign policies, thus trapping the country in what have been described by Western experts as 'muddled' policies in a gray zone of uncertainty and instability.[3]

Ukraine's two decades of independence can be divided into two periods. Whereas national integration prevailed in the 1990s, regional divisions have grown since the 2000 "Kuchmagate" crisis. In Ukraine's first decade, reformist political forces on the center-right, popular in the western-central regions, cooperated with centrist forces popular in eastern-southern Ukraine, to advance Ukraine's "quadruple transition." In the last decade, however, growing regional divisions exploited by both sides of the political fence have divided reformers and, as Olexiy Haran analyzes in his chapter, distracted them from the pursuit of much-needed reforms and Euro-Atlantic integration. As a recent New York University policy paper points out, of the three potential scenarios facing Ukraine up to 2020 the only one leading to an Open Ukraine is that of a grand bargain between eastern and western Ukraine, a 'National Consensus Leading to Reform.'[4] Unless Ukrainian elites overcome their regional divisions, it will be difficult to fashion an elite and public consensus for the reforms outlined in this volume that would facilitate both an Open Ukraine and the country's European integration. Selective use of justice against opposition

---

[3] On Ukraine's "muddle way" see Alexander J. Motyl, "Making Sense of Ukraine," *Harriman Review*, vol. 10, no. 3 (September 1997), pp. 1–7; Dominique Arel, "The Muddle Way," *Current History*, vol. 97, no. 621 (October 1998), pp. 342–46; and Andrew Lushnycky and Mykola Riabchuk, eds., *Ukraine on Its Meandering Path between East and West* (Bern, Switzerland: Peter Lang, 2009).

[4] Center for Global Affairs, New York University, *Ukraine 2020*. http://www.scps.nyu.edu/export/sites/scps/pdf/global-affairs/ukraine-2020-scenarios.pdf.

leaders who are popular in one half of the country, as is being practiced today in Ukraine, only deepens regional divisions and makes reforms and European integration far less likely.

A third factor, an unreformed, largely dysfunctional bureaucracy, stymies efforts at reform even in areas where there is general agreement within the ruling administration and opposition to move forward. Marcin Swiecicki's chapter analyzes the main areas of progress in Ukraine's transition to a market economy and the many areas where reforms remain to be implemented. Rent-seeking clans and oligarchs, most with close ties to the Party of Regions, extract what they can from the existing system without looking ahead to how the economic pie could be expanded for the benefit of themselves and Ukrainian citizens. Economic and social reforms in the last two decades have been piecemeal in response to IMF pressure (1994, 2008-2009, 2010-2011), and failed to meet all the conditions set forth by the IMF in its assistance programs.

Of Ukraine's fourteen governments since 1991, the most reformist was led by Viktor Yushchenko and Yulia Tymoshenko in 2000-2001, when their cooperation in introducing reforms showed signs of progress in moving towards an Open Ukraine. Unfortunately, their cooperation was not evident following the Orange Revolution, when fractious disagreement led to policy stagnation at home and frustration among Ukraine's U.S. and European partners.

A fourth factor, rule of law and corruption, is analyzed in great depth by Bohdan Vitvitsky. No Ukrainian president has seriously fought corruption, and policies in this field have remained virtual rather than real, especially in the energy sector.[5] Transparency International only noted progress in reducing corruption in 2000 and in 2005 during the respective Yushchenko and Tymoshenko governments. Vitvitsky underscores the essential point that rule of law is the foundation of a democratic political system and market economy and therefore of an Open Ukraine. The ten or more criminal cases opened against Tymoshenko, in addition to the charge she was sentenced for, are understood by European and U.S. governments and international

---

[5] T. Kuzio, 'Virtual Reform in a Virtual State,' *Kyiv Post*, May 8, 2003. http://www.kyivpost.com/news/opinion/op_ed/detail/15621/.

organizations as selective use of justice that does not meet democratic rule of law standards

These four factors, together with others, have conspired to prevent the emergence of the type of transformational leadership seen elsewhere in the countries that emerged from the post-communist world over the past two decades. The Orange Revolution inspired hopes both in Ukraine and in the U.S., Canada and Europe that the country had turned an important corner politically that could end the country's immobility and lead to an Open Ukraine and European integration. Kudelia explains how these hopes were dashed, however, as "Orange" authorities maintained symbiotic relationships with the oligarchs, preserved the rent-seeking traditions of their predecessors, used administrative levers to influence the courts and failed to make any substantial progress in integrating Ukraine more deeply into the European mainstream (the one exception being membership of the WTO in May 2008). The "Orange" administration did little to strengthen government accountability and the rule of law, or to place law enforcement structures under democratic control, which has made President Yanukovych's democratic rollback easier.

The fierce competition for power and rents between former allies destroyed the "Orange" coalition and paralyzed policymaking, leading to widespread Ukraine fatigue in Washington, Ottawa and in European capitals. Systemic corruption, which most reports show is growing, has devastated public trust in all branches of government and in the country's leadership making Ukrainians less eager to defend their democracy against attacks upon it by the current leadership. Following Yushchenko's successful visit to Washington in April 2005, the U.S. and NATO sent a strong signal to Ukraine that the country could enter a Membership Action Plan (MAP) towards NATO membership at the November 2006 Riga summit, but the opportunity was missed. Similarly, a second signal by the EU to Ukraine of signing an Association Agreement and Deep and Comprehensive Free Trade Agreement may be frozen again because of domestic political developments. In both cases, NATO and EU integration has been de-railed by divisive policies, disunity, weak political will and lack of strategic vision among Ukrainian elites.

In retrospect, the Yushchenko presidency took the form of what Kudelia describes as "feckless pluralism," a lost opportunity to forge an Open Ukraine that instead paved the way for the country's authoritarian retrenchment under Yanukovych. Democracy as a model of governance has been tarnished in the public eye due to poor governance and the inability of "Orange" leaders to prove they were better and less corrupt than their political opponents. As a consequence, government institutions have been severely weakened; elites are extremely polarized and democratic forces are fractured; and public cynicism about the role of government is pervasive. Ukrainian politicians of all stripes face incredibly high levels of public distrust.[6]

The lack of unity among top government officials in Ukraine and their inability to move beyond an immobile state and implement long-promised reforms has led to Ukraine fatigue among European, Canadian and U.S. leaders. Brussels, Ottawa and Washington are unable to comprehend how the current Ukrainian authorities could chose to prioritize the imprisonment of an opposition leader over the benefits that would accrue to the population at large and country of European integration. Poland, which held the presidency of the European Council in the second half of 2011, is especially disconcerted that its staunch support for Ukraine's European integration has been spurned. As the European Union grapples with the euro-zone crisis, Yanukovych's democratic backsliding offers those Europeans who always were skeptical about EU engagement with Kyiv, and who feared that the Association Agreement was merely the thin edge of a wedge that would lead to membership, a handy excuse to oppose it.

Yanukovych's policies have left Ukraine more isolated internationally, thus creating the conditions for Kyiv's potential drift back into the Russian economic and political orbit. In late April 2010, the coalition headed by Yanukovych railroaded through parliament a 25-year extension of the existing 1997 temporary basing agreement, allowing Russia to base the Black Sea Fleet in Sevastopol until 2042 with the possibility of a five year extension to 2047. As Stephen Larrabee points out, the agreement was ratified without proper parliamentary oversight and in violation of a constitutional provision forbidding for-

---

[6] See numerous surveys by the International Foundations for Electoral Systems: http://www.ifes.org/countries/Ukraine.aspx.

eign bases on Ukrainian territory. In return for extending the base agreement, Russia agreed to lower the price of imported gas by 30 percent from the price determined by the January 2009 contract signed by then Prime Minister Tymoshenko that ended a 17-day European gas crisis. However, due to the falling demand for gas, Russia had already begun renegotiating contracts in Europe and giving customers discounts. Thus, as Frank Umbach writes, the 30% discount simply brought the price negotiated with Yanukovych down to current European average prices. The 2010 gas agreement, and the new agreement signed in late 2011 which lowered the price further, reduces the country's incentive to reform its inefficient and corrupt energy sector, and commits it to buy more gas in future than it may need. At the same time, it increases Ukraine's economic and energy dependence on Russia.

Yanukovych has also reversed the strategy of Ukraine's first three presidents and overturned parliamentary legislation geared toward seeking NATO membership. While distancing himself from NATO, Yanukovych has often expressed his goal of EU membership, and Ukrainian negotiators even demanded that Ukraine's membership goal be fixed in the text of the Association Agreement. EU leaders have failed to offer a membership perspective for Ukraine or any CIS country, however, and relations have focused on negotiation of a DCFTA as part of an Association Agreement, which had been slated for completion by December 2011. Initialing of the Association Agreement was to have been undertaken at the December 19, 2011 EU-Ukraine summit in Kyiv followed by the European Council signing of the agreement in 2012 and recommendation for its ratification by the European Parliament and 27 EU member state parliaments.

While initialing may go ahead, it is unlikely that signing and especially ratification will follow. The trial and conviction of Tymoshenko is the major obstacle to the agreement entering into force.

As the 2012 parliamentary and 2015 presidential elections loom, Yanukovych faces a dilemma. He will either have to accept the possibility of opposition parties gaining substantial representation in the new parliament and being defeated by opposition leaders, or he will have to undertake election fraud of a scale that would surpass that conducted in 2004. The stakes are high. Having established the precedent of criminal persecution of his predecessors, Yanukovych and his allies face the possibility that they could become the target of similar policies if opposition forces record significant gains in 2012 and an opposition candidate wins the presidential election in 2015. Unless Yanukovych is prepared to change course and embark on reforms that could lead to a more open, prosperous and secure Ukraine, through a grand bargain between eastern and western Ukrainian elites, the temptation to falsify the elections could be irresistibly high, leading to further international isolation.

In short, Ukraine again stands at a critical juncture. The country can continue its slide into autocracy and watch as its chances of integrating into the European mainstream fade. Alternatively, as we argue, the country can move towards an Open Ukraine—an effective democracy governed by the rule of law, free of systemic corruption, with a functioning market economy integrated into a far larger European space of prosperity and stability. Actions taken at home and abroad can focus this choice and make the consequences clear to Ukraine's leaders.

Chapter One

Politics and Democracy in Ukraine

Serhiy Kudelia

For most of its two decades of independence Ukraine's political regime has been stuck in the "grey zone" between a developed democracy and a consolidated autocracy.[1] The state's attempts to limit the space for independent political activities and consolidate autocratic rule were successfully resisted by mobilized society actors and vocal opposition groups. The Orange Revolution was expected to put an end to Ukraine's "hollow decade" and push it decisively in the European direction. However, the equilibrium of "partial reforms" proved more resilient then observers imagined at the time. The new post-revolutionary authorities avoided costly institutional reforms that would have harmed particularistic interests, but could have strengthened state capacity and promoted democratic consolidation. As a result, Ukraine's political regime under Viktor Yushchenko's presidency turned into 'feckless pluralism'—one variation of "grey zone" politics—marked by broader space for political contestation, but also destructive elite competition and pervasive corruption. This allowed his successor Viktor Yanukovych to reverse quickly the few democratic gains of the Orange Revolution and move Ukraine to a more authoritarian 'dominant-power' model based on the political monopoly of one political force, the Party of Regions.

This chapter will first look at the political legacy of Yushchenko's presidency that prepared ground for an authoritarian revival. It will then analyze key political reversals under Yanukovych focusing on the closure of main arenas for political contestation and enhanced capacity of the new authorities to neutralize civil society mobilization. The chapter will conclude by outlining a set of recommendations on how

---

[1] Thomas Carothers, "The End of the Transition Paradigm," *Journal of Democracy*, Vol. 13, No. 1 (January 2002), pp. 5-21.

to deter Ukraine from turning into a full-blown authoritarian regime and promote its greater political openness.

The Legacies of Yushchenko's Presidency

Yushchenko came to power in January 2005 on the heels of the strongest popular democratic movement in Ukraine's history. It coalesced around the promises to introduce political freedoms, eliminate corruption, end oligarchic influence on politics, establish clear and transparent rules equally applicable to everyone and integrate Ukraine into Euro-Atlantic structures. Most of these promises, however, proved to be mere campaign rhetoric. The new authorities maintained a symbiotic relationship with big business, preserved the rent-seeking traditions of their predecessors, used administrative levers to influence courts and failed to make any substantial progress in relations with NATO and EU. While abstaining from direct coercion of their opponents or attempts at media censorship, they did not introduce any institutional changes that would strengthen government accountability or the rule of law. The fierce competition for power and rents between former allies produced the breakdown of the Orange coalition and a virtual paralysis of policy-making. Frequent changes of government and several attempts by the president to disband the parliament only exacerbated the major deficiencies in governance. In a fashion typical of "feckless pluralism," competing political forces "traded the country's problems from one hapless side to the other."[2] Incessant corruption scandals, which were never properly investigated, contributed to the dramatic decline in public trust in all branches of government and the country's leadership. In 2009 only 6.7% trusted the Cabinet of Ministers, 5.3% trusted the courts, 4.7% trusted the President and 4.2% trusted the parliament.[3] As a result, five years of Yushchenko's presidency became an era of "lost opportunity" for political or economic reforms.[4] This dismal governance failure opened the path for a comeback in 2010 of the Kuchma era officials grouped

---

[2] Carothers, p. 10.

[3] *Stan Koruptsii v Ukraini. Porivnialnyi analiz zagalnonatsional'nyh doslidzhen': 2007-2009* (Kyiv: International Institute for Sociological Studies, 2011), p. 15: http://kiis.com.ua/img/pr_img/20110920_korup/Corruption%20in%20Ukraine_2007-2009_2011_Ukr.pdf, accessed on October 15, 2011.

around the Party of Regions and led by ex-Prime Minister Viktor Yanukovych.

Five legacies of Yushchenko's presidency made possible Ukraine's authoritarian reversal under Yanukovych. Firstly, democracy as a model of governance has been tarnished in the public perception due to the poor governance record of democratic forces. According to 2009 Pew Research poll, Ukrainians had the lowest support for a multiparty system and one of the lowest levels of satisfaction with democracy in Europe.[5] Only 30% of Ukrainians approved of a shift to a multiparty system and 70% said they were dissatisfied with democracy. Also, less then half believed in the importance of the freedom of speech and free media. The one democratic principle Ukrainians valued most—a fair judicial system—was also the one that remained a distant ideal even under Yushchenko's presidency.[6]

His second legacy has been a severe weakening of all state institutions exacerbated by the semi-presidential model that fueled infighting among political elites. The constitutional amendments introduced in December 2004 produced an overlap of many executive functions between the president and the government. The president's failure to secure a loyal majority in parliament led to the rotation of combative Prime Ministers (Yulia Tymoshenko in 2005 and 2007-10; Yanukovych in 2006-07), who attempted to accumulate additional powers at the expense of the presidency. In response, Yushchenko used his power to suspend government resolutions in order to subordinate the Cabinet of Ministers and regain some influence over policy-making. During his one term Yushchenko tried to stop over hundred government resolutions or five times more then Kuchma vetoed during his ten years in office. Given that he lacked other levers to influence the government's

---

[4] Taras Kuzio, "With or Without Baloha, Yushchenko's Unelectable," *Kyiv Post*, May 28, 2009.

[5] "The Pulse of Europe 2009: 20 Years after the Fall of the Berlin Wall," http://pewglobal.org/2009/11/02/end-of-communism-cheered-but-now-with-more-reservations/, accessed on September 1, 2011.

[6] According to a Pew poll, 67% of Ukrainians believed in the importance of a fair judicial system. For the analysis of Ukraine's judiciary system under Yushchenko see Alexei Trochev, "Meddling with Justice: Competitive Politics, Impunity, and Distrusted Courts in Post-Orange Ukraine," *Demokratizatsiya: the Journal of Post-Soviet Democratization*, Vol. 18, No. 2 (Spring 2010), pp. 122-147.

policies, such as the power to fire disloyal Cabinet members, Yushchenko resorted to the one that had the most destructive effects on government's work. Moreover, with the President maintaining the power to appoint oblast governors the government also faced difficulties implementing its decisions on the local level. As a result, Ukraine's amended constitution, which expanded the role of the parliament and could have potentially strengthened horizontal accountability, was discredited as a recipe for dysfunctional governance.

Yushchenko's third legacy has been further polarization among elite groups and the fracturing of the national-democratic forces. President single-handedly promoted a number of divisive issues, particularly the honoring of the World War II nationalist movement and accelerated integration with NATO. This deepened Ukraine's regional divisions and heightened the intensity of political conflict. Furthermore, Yushchenko also set against himself most of his former allies in the Orange camp by making erratic appointments and entering into suspect deals with shady oligarchs. His attempts to undermine Tymoshenko's government in 2008-2009 produced a series of political crises that led to a final breakdown of the Orange coalition. As a result, public support for a pro-presidential party 'Our Ukraine' dwindled, while many of the President's earlier supporters started their own political parties (Vyacheslav Kyrylenko, Anatoliy Grytsenko, Mykola Katerynchuk) or joined forces with Tymoshenko (Yuriy Lutsenko, Borys Tarasyuk).

Another legacy of Yushchenko's presidency has been the overall alienation of society from the state reflected in rising political apathy and cynicism. This has been partially the result of the economic crisis hitting Ukraine in late 2008, but it also reflected society's sense of powerlessness to affect the status quo. Frequent elections failed to improve the quality of governance or produce new leaders. At the same time, protest actions became largely discredited as a mechanism of change due to a widespread practice of hiring protesters and the lack of impact on government. The rising popularity of the radical nationalist party "Svoboda" ("Freedom") in Western Ukraine in 2009-2010 was another way that voters expressed their disillusionment with the inability of a national-democratic leadership to deliver.[7]

---

[7] Anton Shekhovtsev, "The Creeping Resurgence of the Ukrainian Radical Right? The Case of the Freedom Party," *Europe-Asia Studies*, Vol. 63, No. 2 (March 2011), p. 222.

Finally, the lack of unity among top government officials in Ukraine and their inability to implement promised reforms produced 'Ukraine fatigue' among Western leaders. Despite their general approval of Yushchenko's record on democracy, Ukraine's integration with the EU and the development of strategic partnership with the US have been sidetracked by poor governance and continued corruption on the highest levels of government. With no clear negotiating partner in Kyiv and continuous policy zig-zags, the West could not pursue any coherent policy towards Ukraine.

Ukraine under Yanukovych

Elected in February 2010, Yanukovych inherited a dysfunctional state and a divided society. However, rather than reforming the inefficient bureaucracy, strengthening the rule of law and engaging civil society in policy-making, Yanukovych opted to introduce an authoritarian 'dominant-power' model without precedents in Ukraine's independent history. Even at the height of Kuchma's autocratic rule Ukraine's political regime maintained a competitive nature,[8] allowing political contestation in several key arenas, particularly in the electoral field, the legislature and the media. The opposition could stage mass protests and demonstrations in Kyiv and elsewhere across Ukraine, while parliament could successfully resist some of the president's key initiatives. Moreover, Kuchma's regime was characterized by a limited scope of control over the economy with a diverse distribution of private wealth among business groups outside of the authorities' direct influence. The organization of the political elite under Kuchma was weakened by the lack of a single ruling party that could coordinate the activities of key elite actors. Instead, Kuchma allowed various political parties to engage in bitter competition for patronage and rents. This

---

[8] Steven Levitsky and Lucan Way, "The Rise of Competitive Authoritarianism," *Journal of Democracy*, Vol. 13, No.2 (April 2002), pp. 51-65; Taras Kuzio, "Ukraine's Orange Revolution. The Opposition's Road to Success," *Journal of Democracy*, Vol.16, No. 2 (April 2005), pp. 117-130; and Paul D'Anieri, "The Last Hurrah: The 2004 Ukrainian Presidential Elections and the Limits of Machine Politics," *Communist and Post-Communist Studies*, Vol. 38, No. 2 (June 2005), pp. 231-249.

made it easier for the opposition to attract private funds and encourage elite defections prior to, and during, the Orange Revolution.[9]

By contrast, Yanukovych has sought to manage political contestation, constrain civil society, subordinate the private sector and enhance the organization of the ruling elite. The lessons from Kuchma's failed authoritarianism, the successful example of Russia's relatively stable autocracy and Yanukovych's own experience as a governor of Donetsk (1997–2002) provided the new Ukrainian authorities with an institutional know-how to build a stable, authoritarian regime.

The Parliamentary Arena

Over the first year of Yanukovych's presidency the Ukrainian parliament turned into a rubber-stamp body with minimal political authority. Although the Party of Regions failed to form the majority coalition following 2007 elections after Yanukovych became President his entourage resorted to a mixture of threats and bribery to encourage the defection of several dozen deputies from other factions. A change in the procedural rules for coalition-formation allowed the new ruling party to form a pro-presidential majority in parliament and vote on the new government. The new cabinet included mostly Yanukovych's loyalists from the Party of Regions with his long-standing ally Nikolai Azarov at the helm. The weakness of the two opposition factions in the parliament became further apparent when they failed to prevent the ratification of the Russian-Ukrainian Accords extending Russia's lease of the Black Sea Base in Sevastopol for another 25 years. Finally, October 2010 ruling of the Constitutional Court annulled the 2004 constitutional reforms returning Ukraine to the semi-presidential system of the 1996 constitution, that transferred control over the government from parliament to the president. As a result, Yanukovych could now select and fire the Prime Minister, appoint and dismiss cabinet members as well as veto government resolutions. The president also regained decisive influence over agencies of coercion with his power to dismiss single-handedly any top law-enforcement officials without parliament's consent.

---

[9] Lucan Way, "Authoritarian State-Building and the Sources of Regime Competitiveness in the Fourth Wave. The Cases of Belarus, Moldova, Russia and Ukraine," *World Politics*, Vol. 57, no. 2 (January 2005), pp. 231-261.

With renewed subordination of the government directly to the president the legislature lost much of its earlier political weight.

The pro-presidential parliamentary factions also acquired total control over the legislative process. The Rada's (Parliaments) new procedural rules adopted in October 2010 left opposition factions without any oversight mechanisms to control the government's decision-making and state budget expenditures. They also lost their earlier powers to influence the agenda of parliamentary sessions. The two opposition factions—Bloc of Yulia Tymoshenko (BYuT) and Our Ukraine-Self-Defense (NU-NS)—currently lack strong leadership and remain deeply fractured. They have also been weakened by the jailing of their two leaders Tymoshenko and Lutsenko, which encouraged further defection of their members to the pro-presidential Stability and Reforms coalition.

A strong and independent legislature is vital for jump-starting the reform process in Ukraine. A number of comparative studies have demonstrated that a post-communist countries with a parliamentary system have been most successful in reforming their economies and consolidating democracy.[10] Coalition governments could minimize the influence of rent-seekers on decision-making, prevent the monopolization of the political process and promote consensus-building within the polity.

The Electoral Arena

The electoral process under Yanukovych has been purposefully skewed to favor the ruling party. The new mechanisms to limit the electoral arena included the Rada's legislative innovations that introduced a mixed election system for local councils, expanded the powers of territorial election commissions and adopted new staffing rules for the commissions that benefitted pro-presidential parties in parliament. Although local elections were earlier scheduled for May 2010, parliament voted to postpone them until October 31, 2010. In the mean-

---

[10]Joel Hellman, "Winners Take All: The Politics of Partial Reform in Postcommunist Transitions," *World Politics*, Vol. 50, No. 2 (January 1998), pp. 203-234 and Grzegorz Ekiert, Jan Kubik and Milada Anna Vachudova, "Democracy in the Post-Communist World: An Unending Quest?" *East European Politics and Societies*, Vol. 21, No. 1 (February 2007), pp. 7-30.

time, the pro-presidential majority changed the electoral law reviving the mixed system with half of the seats in the local councils filled by the candidates winning in single-member districts (SMD) and another half based on the closed party-list proportional representation. As a result, while winning 39% of votes across Ukraine on the party list, the Party of Regions acquired the majority of seats in *oblast* and city councils in 10 oblasts and formed majority coalition in another 12 oblasts with the help of SMD deputies. Although most of the candidates (45.7%) winning in single-member races were not affiliated with any political party, they overwhelmingly joined the Party of Regions faction upon entering councils.

The Party of Regions and its allies also had majority control in the territorial electoral commissions where opposition parties were severely underrepresented. Using their expanded powers territorial commissions could refuse the registration of party candidates, fire any commission member and certify election results with the minimum quorum of just three members present. Several local opposition candidates were excluded from the election process in 2010 campaign. The authorities also prevented Tymoshenko's Batkivshchina party from participating in local elections in Kyiv and Lviv *oblasts* by refusing to recognize its new local party chairmen, which helped radical nationalists to gain the absolute majority of seats in the Lviv local council.

The new electoral law pre-approved by the president for the October 2012 parliamentary elections revives a similar mixed electoral system on the national level. It will allow the ruling party to form a pro-presidential majority with the support of non-partisan deputies winning in single-member districts, repeating what already happened in 2002. The draft electoral law also raises the electoral threshold to 5% and bans electoral blocs, which would prevent a broad opposition alliance similar to "Our Ukraine" in 2002 from emerging out of a fractured national-democratic field. Finally, the law preserves a closed party list system, which gives the party leadership exclusive powers to decide the candidates who will represent the party in parliament. According to the conclusions of the Venice Commission, the draft law fails to address several critical areas of concern, particularly it lacks clarity on the possibility of challenging election results, lacks provision for full disclosure of funding sources and the amount of contributions and bans anyone convicted of a criminal offense from participation in the elections. Most importantly, the new electoral law was drafted in a non-transparent manner without any public deliberations or participation of opposition parties and non-governmental organizations, which seriously undermines its legitimacy.

The Judiciary

Yanukovych showed few scruples in using the judicial branch for political purposes. In April 2010 the Constitutional Court confirmed the legitimacy of the new rules of coalition-formation in the legislature that allowed the president to form a loyal parliamentary majority by attracting deputies from opposition factions. This decision was particularly stunning given that the Court issued an opposite ruling less then two years earlier banning individual deputies from joining a majority coalition if their faction ruled against it. Out of eight judges who voted against the April decision, four lost their positions in the run-up to the October court hearings on the 2004 constitutional reforms. All the newly appointed judges of the court voted in favor of annuling the amendments and restoring the Kuchma-era constitution.

Yanukovych also used judicial reform to limit the role of Ukraine's Supreme Court, which was headed by Tymoshenko's ally Vasyl Onopenko. The new July 2010 law on the judiciary transferred most of the Supreme Court's appelate jurisdiction to specialized higher courts, such as a new court for civil and criminal matters, which was controlled by judges loyal to the president. Judicial reform also provided the High Council of Justice, which is run by the president's long-time ally Sergei Kivalov, broad new powers to appoint and remove lower-level judges. As the Council of Europe's Venice Commission noted, given the politicization of the Council this change became a major setback for judicial independence in Ukraine. One particularly progressive element of the law, which received praise from the Venice Commission, was the new procedure for automatic case-assignement. Earlier, the courts' chairmen were in charge of assigning cases to paritucular judges making the whole process non-trasparent and ripe for corruption. However, as the mounting evidence indicates, the automatic system could be circumvanted by running the program several times until the "right" judge is selected.[11]

---

[11]Marta Dyczok, "The Ukrainian Blues (and Yellows)," *The Wall Street Journal*, August 26, 2011.

The failures of the new program for the selection of judges came to the fore in the criminal cases against opposition leaders Tymoshenko and Lutsenko. In both instances the chief judges were relatively inexperienced and had a history of suspect rulings in the past,[12] making them particularly vulnerable to outside political pressure. The two cases also demonstrated new limits on the judiciary. In semi-authoritarian regimes judges can still rule against the interests of the authorities, as was demonstrated by the refusal of Ukraine's Supreme Court to recognize the April 2000 referendum results as binding or by Tymoshenko's release from prison in March 2001 on the court's order.[13] However, there have been no court decisions during Yanukovych's presidency that havecontradicted his personal political interests. The trial of opposition leader Tymoshenko, which the EU's High Representative for Foreign Affairs Catherine Ashton characterized as failing to respect international standards of fairness and independence, only reinforced this trend towards continued manipulation of the judiciary for political purposes.

The President currently exerts political infleunce over the judiciary through the Higher Council of Justice, which is dominated by representatives of the ruling Party of Regions. Hence, the first step towards a genuine judicial indepence would require minimizing the role of the Council in judicial affairs. Its powers to select or discipline judges should be transferred to a non-partisan body comprising of authoritative and experienced judges, such as the High Qualifications Commission. Finally, the President's and Parliament's role in appointing or removing judges should also be limited to mere approval of the Commission's recommendations with few clearly specified exceptions.

Media and Civil Society

Media censorship under Yanukovych has not yet reached the level characteristic of Kuchma's presidency. There is no centralized system of agenda-setting for news coverage on major television channels, which existed under Kuchma in the form of 'temnyky' (talking-points sent by the presidential administration for reporters). However, con-

---

[12]Tetiana Chornovil, "Zlochyny ta pokarannia Rodiona Kireeva," *Ukrainska Pravda*, September 1, 2011.

[13]Levitsky and Way, op. cit., p. 56.

trol over the leading television channels by oligarchic moguls close to Yanukovych has produced a more decentralized system of self-censorship. The news reports provide selective coverage and usually portray opposition activities in a negative light. According a study of seven leading Ukrainian TV channels, over 70% of the news broadcasts in 2011 focused on the authorities and less then 20% mentioned the activities of the opposition.[14] Moreover, the news reports covering the opposition tend to be more critical in tone and less balanced in substance. Pro-government television channels ignored the Western condemnation of the sentencing of Tymoshenko. Rather than banning the opposition all together, talk-show hosts often invite moderate opposition figures with little public following. The one television channel which has maintained its independence—TVi—lost some of its broadcasting licenses in a court dispute with the major TV channel "Inter" owned by Security Service of Ukraine (SBU) Chairman Valeriy Khoroshkovskiy. It was also sidelined in the recent distribution of frequencies for digital broadcasting.

The Presidential Administration also introduced new limits on the journalists' access to the President and high-ranking government officials. Prominent investigative reporters are rarely given a chance to pose direct questions to Yanukovych during his press-conferences, while government officials ignore requests for public information submitted from independent media outlets only pre-selected group of loyal journalists was allowed to participate in a round-table with the President in his private residence outside of Kyiv. Overall, major media outlets in Ukraine have not yet fallen fully under the government's control, but their independence has eroded substantially due to the excessive interference of owners in news coverage. Only print and internet-based media still function as an instrument of accountability and a source of reliable news. Further international assistance to these outlets is vital for assisting the Ukrainian media maintain some degree of independence.

The authorities have used a variety of administrative levers in order to deter the organization of civic actions or increase participation costs for civic activists. The local authorities have renewed the prac-

---

[14]"Telekanaly adresuyut negatyv opozytsii," *Telekrytyka*, July 20, 2011: http://www.media osvita.com.ua/material/2919.

tice of appealing to courts to ban opposition demonstrations or protests. Local courts have banned a number of large protest actions, including the rally against the new tax legislation on the *Maidan* (November 2010), tent cities in support of Tymoshenko in Kyiv, Kharkiv, Odesa and Rivne (July 2011), and opposition demonstrations in the Ukrainian capital on Independence Day (August 2011). The courts' verdicts then became a pretext for the use of *spetsnaz* police units to violently disband protests or prevent the demonstrators from mobilizing. Furthermore, the authorities also pursued criminal actions against leading protest organizers, including prominent opposition figures, charging them with illegal activities and resistance to the law-enforcement. These actions serve to threaten civil society activists and deter the public from wider participation in protest actions. International institutions should step up their criticisms of the Ukrainian authorities in order to prevent further emasculation of civic groups and the closing of public space for independent political action.

State Power

The power of the state apparatus is a key indicator of an incumbents' capacity to resist political challenges.[15] Its main components are the level of control over subordinates and the scope of state activity. State control was particularly weak under Yushchenko as the President lost power to appoint his candidates to most government positions, which often resulted in a refusal to subordinate lower-ranking government officials. The strength of control over subordinates has improved markedly under Yanukovych and he has not revoked any government resolutions, an indication of a renewed informal coordination between the Cabinet and Presidential Administration. Higher elite compliance is partially the result of President's renewed power to appoint and fire government officials on all levels. It has also become possible with the President's reliance on the Party of Regions and which serves as a mechanism to select and test political loyalists.

The degree of state monopolization of economic and political power reflects the existence of autonomous power centers outside of state control. One of the most important factors needed to maintain political competition and a vibrant civil society has been large inde-

---

[15]Way, op. cit., p. 234.

pendent private business. The high level of economic dispersion in Ukraine and the willingness of wealthy business leaders to fund the opposition helped it to wage a successful campaign in 2004.[16] Political preferences of big business remained divided under Yushchenko with major oligarchs backing competing political leaders and presidential candidates in the 2010 elections. After the first year of Yanukovych's presidency, however, wealth has been increasingly concentrated in the hands of the members of the Party of Regions. According to the estimates of the weekly magazine *Korrespondent*, 25 out of the 100 wealthiest Ukrainians are members of the ruling party[17] and their total wealth has been estimated at $31.1 billion. By contrast, there were only two businessmen close to the largest opposition party Batkivshchyna (Fatherland), with a total wealth estimated at $3.2 billion. Most of these funds belong to a billionaire Kostiantyn Zhevago, whose businesses have been recently pressured by the tax inspectors and has resigned from the BYuT (Bloc of Yulia Tymoshenko) parliamemtary faction. All other major funders of Tymoshenko's presidential campaign, such as banker Oleksandr Buriak and car-maker Tariel Vasadze, defected to Yanukovych following his election victory. The current high level of state control over big businesses is likely to increase even further resulting in the complete cooptation of major businessmen into the ruling party.

Elite Organization

Another factor ensuring the sustainability of authoritarian regimes has been the strength of elite organization. Kuchma relied on diverse elite groups with no coherent organizational structure, which made the regime particularly vulnerable to defections and weakened the level of control over subordinates in the regions. Yanukovych's comeback, first as Prime Minister in 2006 and then as President in 2010, became possible largely because of his reliance on the organizational resources of the Party of Regions. His appointment policy reflects the significance of the party's role. The party leadership controls all of the key positions in the Presidential Administration and the Cabinet of

---

[16]Scott Radnitz, "The Color of Money: Privatization, Economic Dispersion, and the Post-Soviet 'Revolutions'," *Comparative Politics*, Vol. 42, No. 2 (April 2010), pp. 127-46.

[17]"Zolotaia Sotnia," *Korrespondent*, June 10, 2011.

Ministers. Azarov, Party of Regions leader, is also the prime minister, while the two Deputy Prime Ministers and the Head of the Presidential Administration are members of the party's highest governing council. Similarly, nineteen out of twenty four chairmen of oblast administrations are members of the Party of Regions. The mergers of the Strong Ukraine party led by Deputy Prime Minister Sergei Tigipko and the People's Party led by Parliamentary Chairman Volodymyr Lytvyn with the Party of Regions would further indicate that the authorities intend to consolidate a dominant-power system in Ukraine.

In the dominant-power systems a single political force maintains strict control over key state resources and a commanding presence in all power branches and on all levels of government.[18] The ruling party is also a focal point coordinating the activities of lower-level officials, which allows for a more efficient use of administrative resources in the interests of the ruling elite. Finally, the existence of a single party of power ensures the redistribution of rents among loyalists, creates a clear mechanism for career promotion and raises the costs of defection to the opposition. The Party of Regions has thus turned into the country's largest patronage network, which limits political competition by controlling the distribution of government positions and providing privileged power access to its members. However, the exclusion of other political groups from the decision-making adversely affects the quality of reform proposals and weakens their public support across Ukraine.

Know-How

The final factor contributing to the stability of an autocratic regime has been the skill with which autocratic leaders can neutralize the opposition and consolidate their power. Yanukovych's team drew lessons both from its own political defeat in 2004 and from the examples of neighboring autocracies in Russia and Belarus. There are five main elements of a successful autocratic model that Yanukovych may try to implement in Ukraine. First of all, reliance on a dominant political party helps to eliminate 'rapacious individualism' that led to persistent political conflicts throughout the last two decades of

---

[18]Carothers, op. cit. p. 12.

Ukrainian independence.[19] Second, political control over big business undercuts funding for the opposition and limits negative coverage in the media. Third, consistent use of excessive coercion against protesters helps to deter anti-incumbent mobilization by civil society. Fourth, jailing of key opposition leaders weakens the opposition movement and demoralizes opposition supporters. Fifth, subordination of autonomous institutional power bases such as parliament, local government and the courts marginalizes the opposition leaving it devoid of any legal means to mount a successful challenge to autocratic incumbents. During the first two years of his presidency Yanukovych has been persistently implementing each of the five elements of the model described in this chapter.

In addition, there has been a new element in autocracy-building possibly introduced in Ukraine. The wide media promotion of the radical right nationalist party Svoboda (Liberty) that won the 2010 local elections in the three Galician *oblasts* of Western Ukraine by sidelining mainstream national-democratic parties may indicate that the authorities were informally backing its campaign. The strengthening of an ultra-nationalist party in the region, which was once a stronghold of the democratic opposition, further weakens democratic forces and helps to rally Yanukovych's voters in Eastern and Southern Ukraine around the Party of Regions who felt threatened by Ukrainian nationalism.

Policy Recommendations

The first step to a goal of an Open Ukraine is reviving the parliament's role in choosing candidates for Cabinet of Ministers positions and giving it strong oversight powers over the executive, particularly by establishing a clear procedure for impeaching the president. The internal rules for coalition-formation should prioritize party factions over individual deputies and provide for the majority coalition based solely on parties that entered parliament. There should also be a strict enforcement of the rules requiring deputies to vote individually and disclose their personal income declarations. In addition, opposition

---

[19]Lucan Way, "Rapacious Individualism and Political Competition in Ukraine, 1992-2004," *Communist and Post-communist Studies*, Vol. 38, No. 2 (June 2005), pp. 191-205.

factions in parliament should be guaranteed chairmanship positions in the committees overseeing the law-enforcement, judiciary, media freedoms and budgetary policies and the power to nominate the head of the Accounting Chamber.

An Open Ukraine requires an electoral law that would ensure a level playing field for competing political parties and their fair representation in parliament. Mixed electoral systems prevents this by skewing election results in favor of the ruling party and opening the possibility for distorting society's aggregate political preferences. Proportional representation with open party lists has proven to be the most successful electoral model for post-communist states as it engages citizens in selecting their representatives and minimizes the possibility for usurping power by one political force. It would also help to develop Ukraine's nascent party political system, which still remains highly volatile. Legislation should also minimize the ability of electoral commissions to interfere with the electoral process and make arbitrary decisions that could distort the election outcome. In addition, targeted assistance by international actors, particularly the funding of independent media and monitoring groups, should help to neutralize the structural advantages of the incumbency in Ukraine.

A strategy of moving Ukraine out of its current 'grey zone' and becoming an Open Ukraine should be based on five policy proposals:

1) Support Dialogue

By monopolizing political space and marginalizing the opposition the Ukrainian authorities undermine the reform process and weaken public trust in policy outcomes. Hence, international organizations and Western governments should encourage active involvement of opposition parties and leading NGOs in the process of drafting reform strategies and policy proposals. Opposition factions in parliament should also be granted greater oversight powers in order to control budget expenditures and the functioning of the law-enforcement bodies. The President and Prime Minister should rely on consensus-building mechanisms and public dialogue in pushing their legislative initiatives through parliament. Without the opposition's ability to shape the policy-making process and influence the legislative process Ukraine is unlikely to fulfill its obligations under the Deep and Comprehensive Free Trade Agreement with the EU.

2) Advocate Institutional Reforms

The European governments, particularly representatives of post-communist countries, should advocate targeted institutional reforms aimed at limiting the powers of the presidency, increasing the government's accountability to parliament and strengthening oversight agencies, such as an independent anticorruption bureau, accounting chamber, the office of the ombudsman and the financial regulatory body. Another major area of reform is depoliticizing the judiciary and the civil service, which are still dominated by vested political and business interests. This requires introducing a transparent and clear mechanism for hiring and promoting judges and civil servants.

3) Leverage External Pressure

The U.S. and EU demonstrated impressive unanimity in condemning the trial and the conviction of opposition leader Tymoshenko and issued strong demands for her release. However, Western governments and organizations should act in concert not only in condemning the persecution of the opposition, but also in developing a set of measures that would raise the cost of further undemocratic steps for the Ukrainian authorities. Such measures should include the suspension of Ukraine's membership in the Council of Europe, introducing visa bans for officials responsible for ordering the crackdown against protesters or persecution of the opposition, freezing negotiations on DCFTA and limiting bilateral contacts with top Ukrainian leadership.

At the same time, the EU should make it clear that Ukraine could receive a formal membership offer if it returns to the democratic path. EU conditionality has been most effective when target countries have received a clear promise of EU membership. As long as the EU avoids extending this promise to Ukraine, the Ukrainian government will have little incentive to undertake political and economic reforms. The EU's promise to accept Ukraine as a credible candidate for EU membership may strengthen its authority within Ukrainian society and deter the country's ruling elite from further rollback of democratic freedoms.

4) Target Support to Civil Society

The main source of threat for the sustainability of dominant-power systems has been an independent civil society capable of monitoring the authorities and publicizing their transgressions. The U.S. and EU should provide most of their financial aid to support national and local

NGOs and media outlets that ensure government accountability on all levels.

5) Push for Democratic Elections in October 2012

Western governments and international organizations should stress the critical importance of a free and fair parliamentary campaign in 2012 early in the process and quickly react to even minor violations of democratic procedures. They should also form a political monitoring team consisting of prominent public figures with a strong reputation in Ukraine. This group should visit the country on a bimonthly basis and provide interim assessments of the electoral process. It is important for the group to visit all of Ukraine's regions and meet local officials to convey the special importance of the upcoming parliamentary election. Finally, international organizations should provide technical assistance in training election observers and electoral commission members representing all political parties. The ability of the new parliament to legislate a progressive reform package critically depends on the legitimacy of the election itself and its recognition as free and fair by all major political actors. A new democratically elected parliament could also act as a stronger counterweight against the excessive political dominance of the President.

Conclusions

Ukraine's competitive authoritarian system, which took the form of 'feckless pluralism' under Yushchenko, has been gradually transformed into a 'dominant-power' model under Yanukovych. Its main characteristics include (1) limiting political contestation through coercion and administrative interference; (2) monopolization of power by the presidency that controls other branches; (3) restricting access to public offices exclusively for members of the ruling party. Heightened repression against the opposition, however, indicates that the political regime in Ukraine risks degenerating into a full-blown autocracy. This trend may accelerate with further decline of popular support behind Yanukovych and his increasing international isolation. Already in the first year of his presidency Yanukovych's approval rating dropped from 40% in May 2010 to 9.7% in June 2011.[20] The loss of support for

---

[20] "Idol Sdulsia," *Korrespondent*, July 22, 2011.

Yanukovych has been most substantial in his core electoral areas of Eastern and Southern Ukraine.

If public support behind the president remains at the same low level, Yanukovych will face a dilemma in the run-up to 2012 parliamentary elections. He will either have to accept the possibility of opposition parties gaining substantial representation in the new parliament, or he will have to use administrative levers to an unprecedented degree to interfere with the election process and rig the election results. However, if the Party of Regions understands that it would fail to win fairly the latter option may be increasingly likely. First, Yanukovych needs to have a compliant legislature with a significant pro-presidential majority in order to secure re-election in 2015. Parliament proved to be an effective institutional forum for the opposition in the run-up to the presidential election in 2004. It provided opposition leaders with immunity from persecution and allowed them to resist some of Kuchma's key legislative initiatives. Moreover, the opposition's strong showing in 2002 demonstrated the vulnerability of the existing regime, which encouraged further political resistance and elite division. At the same time, the stakes of the 2015 presidential election for the ruling elites has increased substantially so they can no longer afford to lose it. Having established the precedent of criminal persecution of his predecessors, Yanukovych and his allies are now likely to become the target of similar actions if an opposition candidate wins election in 2015. Moreover, with executive powers again concentrated in the presidency the next presidential race will turn into yet another winner-takes-all contest. Hence, the current ruling party will risk losing most of its influence over decision-making if the president changes.

Finally, the experience of the Orange Revolution may have taught Yanukovych's oligarchic entourage that any transfer of power to an opposition may also threaten their ownership rights and lead to a redistribution of property. Given that the key oligarchic groups within the Party of Regions have gained major new assets under Yanukovych's presidency, they will be keen on maintaining him in office at any cost as long as he could guarantee the safety of their property. Another lesson Yanukovych may have drawn from his campaign in 2004 is that unless the opposition is marginalized early on it can turn into a serious challenge at a later stage. Hence, real presidential contenders, such as Tymoshenko, need to be excluded from the election process prior to the launch of the presidential race. This will be much easier if they end up being either in jail or outside parliament.

International efforts to deter Ukraine's further backsliding should combine the threat of costly sanctions against the ruling elite with demands for greater involvement of opposition parties in policy-making and a targeted assistance to key actors in civil society and calls for specific institutional reforms that would lead to a more balanced political system in Ukraine. Outside pressure on the Ukrainian authorities clearly has its limits and the main brunt of responsibility for the evolution of Ukraine's political regime lies on domestic actors. However, as the Orange Revolution also demonstrated, Western influence can restrict the range of options available for the authorities in fighting the opposition and weaken the internal legitimacy of some of the government's anti-democratic policies. Given that the balance of power has been strongly in favor of the authorities, a harder line by the West combined with a promise of EU membership may strengthen those civil society actors and opposition figures who have been resisting Ukraine's autocratic reversal.

Chapter Two

National Integration and National Identity in Ukraine

Olexiy Haran

The issue of regionalism is extremely important in understanding Ukrainian politics and geopolitics. Most of Ukraine suffered from three centuries of overt Russification (culminating in the 1876 Ems Decree that banned all publications in the Ukrainian language as well as public readings and stage performances) and subtle Russification in the Soviet Union, which was especially prevalent in south and east of the country.

On the other hand, most of Western Ukraine was part of the Austrian-Hungarian empire before 1918, then part of Poland in the interwar period, and annexed by the Soviet Union in 1939-1940. This region underwent Russification for only about 40 years and, therefore, in its traditions, political culture, geopolitical orientations this region is quite similar to the three Baltic states.[1]

In this situation, independent Ukraine faces the challenge to build simultaneously not only a democracy and market economy but also state institutions, and a modern civic nation; that is, a "quadruple transition."[2] The fundamental nature of such a transition ensures it is more difficult compared to Poland, Hungary, and the Baltic countries, an important fact which is quite often overlooked by Western policymakers. In a nutshell, national integration is an important precursor for successful introduction of democratic and economic reforms.

---

[1] It is important to stress that since 2004, not only Western but also Central Ukraine votes for Orange and post-Orange political forces.

[2] See Taras Kuzio, "The National Factor in Ukraine's Quadruple Transition," *Contemporary Politics*, Vol.6. No. 2 (June 2000), pp. 143-164.

Towards the end of the Soviet regime, in 1990, only 45% of pupils studied in Ukrainian, and in higher education about 90% of subjects were taught in Russian. In independent Ukraine, the Russification of education has been halted. Nevertheless, in 2009 18% of pupils were studying in Russian, and if one considers those who study the Russian language as a subject the figure increases to more than 45%.[3]

In higher education, 12% of Ukraine's students (as of 2009) studied in Russian, but the actual figure is higher (it is difficult to determine exact figures as one professor can teach in Russian, another in Ukrainian). The numbers for higher education in Ukrainian drop dramatically in the eastern and southern regions. In the Crimea, Ukrainians comprise 24% of the population, but only 7% of pupils are taught in Ukrainian. In vocational schools in the Crimea all subjects are taught in Russian, 90% of university students study in Russian, and in the Donbas (Donetsk and Luhansk *oblasts*)—50%. More than 40% of all books in circulation in Ukraine are in Russian (as of 2009) and given the large volume of book imports from Russia the figure rises to 90%. Two-thirds of the country's newspapers and 90% of journals, and half of TV programs are in Russian.[4]

The Russian language still dominates in the business sphere and mass entertainment. Despite articles in the 1996 Constitution, which stipulates Ukrainian is the only official state language, many deputies do not bother to learn Ukrainian and continue to speak Russian in parliament. Therefore, making Russian a second state language, as some politicians (including Viktor Yanukovych as candidate for president in 2004 and 2010) advocate, would threaten the existence of the Ukrainian language.

In the late 1980s, when Ukraine was on the path to independence, there were attempts by the KGB and elements within the Communist Party to halt this by making territorial claims on Kyiv. The pretext that was used was the claim that current Ukrainian borders were formed during World War II (as a result of the Soviet invasion of Poland and the threat of force against Romania following the Molo-

---

[3] Most figures on the language situation are taken from *Dzerkalo Tyzhnia*, August 15, 2009 and September, 25, 2010.

[4] Ibid.

tov-Ribbentrop Pact). Territorial claims were not dominant in the political life of most of Ukraine's neighbors. In their turn, the leaders of the Ukrainian state and its national-democratic opposition were in favor of the principle of inviolability of postwar borders. This principle is seen as a sine qua non of Ukrainian foreign policy and all Ukrainian presidents have supported the territorial integrity of Georgia and Moldova.[5] In September 2008, Yanukovych and the Party of Regions did though support Russia's recognition of South Ossetian and Abkhaz independence through resolutions in the Ukrainian and Crimean parliaments (the former failed but the latter was adopted).

Despite predictions on the eve of Ukrainian independence based on the depth of Russification of eastern Ukraine, the country did not split even in the most difficult crisis year in 1993 when hyper-inflation soared to 10,000%. Polls taken in 1994 showed that only 1% of respondents in Lviv and 5% in Donetsk (the main cities in the west and the east of Ukraine, respectively) wanted Ukraine to cease to exist as a united nation. According to polls conducted by the Kyiv International Institute for Sociology, after a short decline in 1993 the number of those who support Ukraine's independence has returned to the level of the 1991 referendum result.[6]

The risk of ethnic confrontation within Ukraine diminishes as ethno-linguistic boundaries are blurred, and the Russian and Ukrainian languages are closely related. In fact, the very division of Russian and Ukrainian-language speakers is to a certain extent exaggerated because most of the population is bilingual. The younger generation of Ukrainians knows Russian even if half of them do not study it at school because Russian TV programs are broadcast in Ukraine and most radio programs in Ukraine are still conducted in Russian or in both languages.

As for the question of citizenship, Ukrainian leaders adopted in October 1991 the "zero option" where everyone living in Ukraine was

---

[5] Moldovans comprise only 32% of the self-proclaimed Transnistrian Moldovan Republic, while Russians make up 30% of the population and Ukrainians 29%; before 1940 this region was the Moldovan Autonomous SSR within the Ukrainian SSR.

[6] Valerii Khmelko, *Suverenitet yak zahalnonatzionalna tzinnist: sotziolohichnyj aspekt.* http://www.kiis.com.ua/pub/2011/sverenitet.pdf.

eligible for citizenship without any pre-conditions. Thus, Ukrainian citizens' socio-economic and political opportunities were not limited or circumscribed by ethno-linguistic criteria. In fact, Ukraine stands in contrast to many other former Soviet republics in that it gained its independence peacefully and without interethnic conflict. This was a result of firstly, a compromise between the national-democratic opposition and national-communists and secondly, tolerant interaction between *Rukh* (the Ukrainian Popular Movement established in 1989) and ethnic minorities.[7] In its preamble, Ukraine's 1996 Constitution defined "the Ukrainian people" as "citizens of Ukraine of all nationalities."

Thus, modern Ukrainian civic nationalism is based upon territorial, not ethnic, criteria and "inclusive" rather than "exclusive" citizenship. The results of the 2001 census (the first to be held in independent Ukraine) showed a slow Ukrainization of Russophone Ukrainians. Compared to the 1989 Soviet census, the number of ethnic Ukrainians increased from 72.7% to 77.8 % while the number of ethnic Russians decreased from 22.1% to 17.3 %, which was signified a return to the ethnic composition of Ukraine found in 1959 Soviet census.

But, the number of those who consider Russian as their "mother tongue" is higher—29.6% and the Russian language still dominates in the eastern and southern regions of the country. Russian-speaking politicians do not feel excluded from the political process in Kyiv and they feel it is more realistic to compete for power and resources in Kyiv rather than in Moscow. Ukraine's independence elevated the status of what had previously been a provincial Soviet republican elite and became the basis for political and business elites irrespective of the language they speak.[8] Ukraine is also regionally and politically diverse which prevents a single political force to monopolize power (or "pluralism by default").

---

[7] Many Jewish dissidents supported Ukrainian dissidents and the creation of Rukh. In turn, Rukh issued a special appeal to Jews, Russians, and Crimean Tatars and established a Council of Nationalities within Rukh.

[8] Characteristically, Ukraine's second President, Leonid Kuchma (1994–2004), relearned Ukrainian (which he had forgotten during his years at university and in the military-industrial complex). Kuchma published a book in Russian and Ukrainian titled *Ukraine Is not Russia* in which he explained why the Russian language cannot receive state status.

Although the electoral divide between the south and the east, on the one hand, and west and the center of Ukraine, on the other, has been evident in every election since 1990 (the only exception is the 1999 presidential election), there are signs that major players are moving into regions that have traditionally supported their opponents. At the same time, radical nationalist forces (both Russian and Ukrainian) have not received votes above the 3% parliamentary threshold.

Russian Influence and Polarization of the Country Since 2004

Despite three centuries of shared existence in one state with Russia, Ukrainian politics cannot be explained by its intertwined history and culture (or the "clash of civilizations" approach according to which only Western Ukraine belongs to Western civilization) or even by its economic dependence on Russia. Ukrainian politics is the result of the correlation of domestic political forces and the position of the Ukrainian elites.

Moscow and Kyiv viewed the future of the Commonwealth of Independent States (CIS), established on December 8, 1991, from opposite perspectives—as "reintegration" or a "civilized divorce," respectively. Ukraine has not ratified the CIS Charter and therefore, despite being one of its founding states, Ukraine is not formally a member of the CIS. Ukraine also refused to sign the 1992 Tashkent Treaty on Collective Security and Kyiv only has observer status in the Eurasian Economic Community which was launched in 2000.

During Leonid Kuchma's 1994 election campaign he referred several times to the so-called 'Eurasian space.' Two central issues in his campaign were increasing Ukraine's cooperation with Russia, first of all in the economic sphere, and granting official status for the Russian language. However, very soon after his election victory Kuchma pursued policies that strengthened the Ukrainian state to a greater extent than Ukraine's first President Leonid Kravchuk. He defeated separatist forces in the Crimea and in 1997 signed both the Treaty on Friendship, Cooperation and Partnership with Russia (which finally recognized Ukraine's borders!) and NATO-Ukrainian Charter on Distinctive Partnership. Balancing between Russia and the West and pursuing a policy of "multi-vector diplomacy," Kuchma pursued integration of Ukraine with the West while cooperating with the CIS. While distancing himself from his predecessor, whose policies he judged to be "nationalistic," Kuchma at the same time had to take into consideration the position of those who had voted for Kravchuk in western and central Ukraine.

One of the main reasons for Viktor Yushchenko's election in 2004 were slogans common to the whole country that appealed to European values, social justice, rule of law, and struggle against corruption. Kuchma's administration did everything possible to prevent Yushchenko from winning the 2004 elections by presenting him as a radical nationalist who would "oppress" the Russian-speaking population, whereas Yanukovych was portrayed as a great friend of Russia. Yanukovych's Russian and Ukrainian election consultants also promoted the idea of a "schism" in Ukraine between the "nationalistic" West and "industrial" East, depicting Yushchenko in fascist uniform or Ukraine divided into three segregated parts. They also launched an anti-Western, anti-American campaign. The Russian president and Russian election consultants openly supported the Yanukovych campaign, and President Putin twice congratulated Yanukovych on his falsified victory. The country emerged from the 2004 elections extremely polarized with tensions that had already built up between national democratic and Russophone political parties on the increase since the November 2000 Kuchmagate crisis.

Although the "Russian factor" continues to play an important role in Ukrainian domestic politics, Moscow could not prevent Yushchenko's victory in 2004 or the 2007 pre-term elections which removed Yanukovych as prime minister.

Ukraine's economic dependence on Russia has also decreased. Although Russia remains the main trading country for Ukraine, its proportion of Ukrainian trade declined dramatically from 47.5 % in 1994 to 23.05% in pre-crisis 2008. Exports to Russia fell from 37.4 % in 1994 to 23.5% in 2008, and imports from 58.1 % to 22.7%. But in absolute figures the trading situation is different as trade with Russia fell from $17.8 billion in 1994 to $11.7 billion, but then increased in 2004 to $17.7 billion, and $35.2 billion in 2008. Therefore, contrary to what Russian leaders say about the "anti-Russian" nature of the Orange administration which allegedly opposed cooperation with

Russia, trade doubled from 2004 to 2008. Ukrainian exports to Russia grew from $5.9 billion to $15.7 billion (that is in 2.7 times) and imports from $11.8 billion to $19.4 billion.[9]

Despite the good and growing economic interaction between Ukraine and Russia an ideological war continued unabated with Moscow continuing to wage massive propaganda campaigns against Ukraine to discredit its democratic experiment. As an example, on May 19, 2009, Russian President Dmitrii Medvedev issued a decree establishing "a Presidential Commission to combat efforts to reinterpret history in ways that damage Russia's interests."[10] Russian propaganda continued in the Soviet tradition of portraying the Ukrainian national liberation movement as 'fascist and anti-semitic'.[11]

As a result of such campaigns, according to a poll conducted by the Russian Levada Center in January-February 2009, 62% of Russians viewed Ukraine in a negative way and Ukraine rose to third on the list of "unfriendly states" after the U.S. and Georgia. At the same time, 90% of Ukrainians retained a positive attitude towards Russia as there was no concerted, state-led anti-Russian campaign by the Yushchenko administration.[12]

President Yushchenko:
Good Slogans, Counterproductive Policies

Yushchenko's accent on issues of social justice in the 2004 campaign helped to overcome the anti-Western stereotypes and polarizing strategies of his opponents. Following his victory Ukraine needed long-awaited reforms, including unpopular ones and it was important to show that new leaders were fighting corruption at the highest levels

---

[9] The data is taken from official sites www.ukrstat.gov.ua and www.me.gov.ua.

[10] Commission members included the head of the Presidential Administration along with the chief of staff of the Armed Forces, the deputy minister of Foreign Affairs, the deputy secretary of the National Security Council, representatives from the Foreign Intelligence Service, Federal Security Service, and other ministries.

[11] Moscow promoted this stereotype in the Western media as well. See, for example, Moses Fishbein, "The Jewish Card in Russian Special Operations against Ukraine," http://maysterni.com/publication.php?id=35257.

[12] *Dzerkalo Tyzhnia*, February 27, 2010.

and within their own 'inner circle'. Such a public perception would have given them the moral authority to ask Ukrainians to 'tighten their belts'. However, the fight against corruption remained on paper and virtual, as it was under Kuchma and remains the case under the Yanukovych administration.

If reforms had been successful, it would have been possible to raise issues which otherwise would not normally receive sufficient support in the country. On the contrary, when in 2008 Yushchenko's ratings declined to 3-5% it was counter-productive to raise the issue of entering NATO's Membership Action Plan (MAP) merely serving to play into the hands of the opposition which increasingly mobilized around anti-Western slogans.

Paradoxically, support for Ukrainian membership in NATO was higher under Kuchma than under Yushchenko. Polls by the Kyiv-based Razumkov Center for Economic and Political Studies showed that in June 2002 the numbers of those who supported joining NATO and those against were nearly equal—approximately 32% each. In July 2009, at the end of Yuschenko's term, only 20% supported NATO membership while 59% opposed this step.[13] Under Yushchenko, the agreement on Ukraine's accession to WTO was finalized and ratified in 2008. But as there were no economic successes within the country, the step was used by the opposition to blame Orange forces "for selling out Ukraine to the West."

Yanukovych mobilized the Party of Regions and eastern Ukrainian Russophone voters against Yushchenko's policies in support of European and Euro-Atlantic integration, respect for Ukrainian history, culture, and language, the need to overcome divisions in Ukrainian Orthodoxy, and mutual respect in Ukrainian-Russian relations. Con-

---

[13]http://razumkov.org.ua/eng/poll.php?poll_id=46. The figure of 32% was a good launch for an informational campaign compared with some Central-Eastern European countries (i.e., Slovakia or Bulgaria) or Spain (when it joined NATO in 1982 public support stood at only 18%). The decrease in public support can be explained by an intensive anti-Western, anti-American campaign supported by Russia and key figures in Kuchma's entourage in the 2004 elections. It is important, however, to stress that up to 90% of Ukrainian security experts are in favor of joining NATO. While disapproving NATO membership 53% of Ukrainians, at the same time, do not consider NATO to be a threat (according to an April 2009 Razumkov Center poll).

trary to the lessons of the 2004 election campaign, when Yushchenko avoided polarizing issues, his presidency and 2010 presidential campaign deeply divided Ukrainian society. In the 2010 elections he received only 5% of the vote and fifth place.

The paradox is that negotiations with the EU for an Association Agreement and Deep and Comprehensive Free Trade Agreement (DCFTA) were boosted only *after* Orange forces lost the 2010 presidential elections and Ukraine under Yanukovych suffered from democratic regression. Therefore, if the negotiations will end successfully it would be the new anti-Orange regime which could claim credit for Ukraine's European integration.

Federalization or Real Local Self-Government?

The idea of federalization for Ukraine was put forward in 1989 by, among others, Vyacheslav Chornovil, a former dissident and then the head of Rukh. However, during Ukraine's drive to independence the Soviet authorities tried to use this idea to polarize the country and mobilize separatist movements. During the first years of Ukrainian independence it became clear that federalization, attractive as a model for a democratic and multicultural society, could encourage centrifugal tendencies in Ukraine. Therefore, Chornovil very soon changed his initial position and dropped his support. The 1996 constitution did not include the idea of federalization or Russian as a state language. National-democrats, pro-business centrists and the moderate left-in parliament joined forces to adopt the constitution.

During and after the Orange Revolution the Party of Regions also used the idea of federalization to secure its position in its electoral strongholds, to challenge the Orange authorities in Kyiv and also as an election campaign slogan. Given the regional polarization of the country, the absence of administrative-territorial reform and, therefore, a weak financial basis for self-government, federalization could lead not to the development of self-government but to regional "feudalization" of the country. The key issue is to strengthen self-government at the local level: village, town, *rayon* (district).

The country's main political forces agree on the necessity of this step although characteristically, the Party of Regions has after coming

Table 1. Would You Like to Have Your Region Separated From Ukraine and Joined to Another State?

Percent

	West	Center	South	East
Yes	3.4	1.4	11.6	10.4
No	91.3	93.1	75.1	77.9
Difficult to answer	5.3	5.5	13.3	11.7

The poll was taken by the Razumkov Center on May 31 – June 18, 2007. 10956 respondents aged above 18 years were polled in all regions of Ukraine. The sample theoretical error does not exceed 1% (www.razumkov.org.ua/eng/poll.php?poll_id=318)

Ukraine's regions are defined as follows: South — Autonomous Republic of Crimea; Odesa, Kherson, and Mykolaiv oblasts; Center — Kyiv; Vinnytsia, Zhytomyr, Kyiv, Kirovohrad, Poltava, Sumy, Khmelnytsky, Cherkasy, and Chernihiv oblasts; West – Volyn, Zakarpattia, Ivano-Frankivsk, Chernivtsi oblasts; East – Dnipropetrovsk, Donetsk, Zaporizhzhia, Luhansk, and Kharkiv oblasts.

to power avoids mentioning "federalization" in its program. It is important to stress that Ukrainian surveys and polls show that separatist ideas were overwhelmingly rejected throughout the whole country (see table 1).

Crimean Autonomy

The August 2008 Russian invasion of Georgia raised again the issue if Russia can play the separatist card in Crimea as it is the only region in Ukraine where ethnic Russians comprise a majority of the population (58%). It is also the historic land of Crimean Tatars, who were deported by Stalin in 1944 to Central Asia and were only allowed to return to the peninsula after 1989 and today constitute 12% of the Crimea's population. Russia's Black Sea naval base in Sevastopol, extended in April 2010 until 2042-2047, remains an instrument of pressure on Ukraine. The Russian consulate has been issuing passports to Ukrainian citizens in Odessa and Crimea, although dual citizenship is prohibited in Ukraine. Nevertheless, it would be premature to extrapolate the "South Ossetian/Abkhazian" scenario to the Crimea.

The rights of ethnic Russians are not under threat in the Crimea (although this is often raised by Russia and pro-Russian forces in Crimea). It is the Ukrainian language and culture that need state support in the Crimea, not Russian (see above). According to the March 2011 poll by the Razumkov Center, 70% of Crimeans consider Ukraine as their Motherland. For the Crimean elites (most of whom are members of all-Ukrainian parties) it is much more profitable to stay within Ukraine and to negotiate with both Kyiv and Moscow. If the Crimea was part of authoritarian Russia it would lose this bargaining position.

The position of the Crimean Tatars is crucial for the future of Crimea and regional stability. Since the end of the 1980s, Rukh and the Crimean Tatars have supported each other. Crimean Tatar leaders were elected to the Ukrainian parliament within Rukh and subsequently on the list of the Yushchenko's Our Ukraine bloc.

But, if Crimean Tatars feel their rights are not protected, first of all in being given land to build homes, this could strengthen radicals outside the Mejlis (the Crimean Tatar parliament), which for decades has managed to maintain the movement as a moderate and non-violent force. In general, Ukraine's tolerant attitude towards Crimean Tatars is in sharp contrast to the spread of anti-Islamic rhetoric in Russia.

Finally, any large-scale conflict over the Crimea would provoke a strong reaction from the international community, to a far greater degree than that which happened in South Ossetia. However, Moscow could exploit the situation in the Crimea to destabilize the region in order to pressure Kyiv and hinder Ukraine's Euro-Atlantic integration. That is what happened when Ukraine sought a NATO Membership Action Plan in 2008, after which anti-NATO demonstrations were organized in the Crimea. Hardliners in Russia could organize clashes between Crimea's ethnic Russians and Crimean Tatars over land or with Ukrainian nationalist organizations over the Sevastopol Black Sea Fleet naval base.

Religious Divisions: The Split in Ukrainian Orthodoxy

Most Ukrainian believers (about 2/3) are members of Orthodox churches. The Greek Catholic Church (which was underground from 1945-1990) is concentrated in Western Ukraine and comprises about 1/5 of religious believers.[14] There are also Roman Catholic, Protestant, Judaic and Muslim believers in Ukraine.

---

[14]See, the 2006 poll by the Razumkov Center at www.uceps.org/ukr/poll.php?poll_id=300.

The Russian Orthodox Church in Ukraine split after Ukraine became independent leading to the emergence of the Ukrainian Orthodox Church–Kyiv Patriarchate (UOC-KP) which supports the idea of an autocephalous Ukrainian Orthodox Church independent from Moscow. However, this church is not recognized by other canonical Orthodox Churches nor by the Ukrainian Orthodox Church under the Moscow Patriarchate (UOC-MP), which, in terms of the number of parishes, remains the largest church in Ukraine.

The UOC-MP enjoys autonomy, including the right to form its own Synod and appoint bishops without formal approval of the Moscow Patriarch. Some of its bishops support the idea of a united, autocephalous Ukrainian Orthodox Church. Between 2007 and 2009, the UOC-MP and Kyiv Patriarchate opened a cautious dialogue which was cancelled after Yanukovych was elected. In November 2008, the UOC-MP Synod pronounced the 1933 artificial famine in Ukraine (*holodomor*) as a genocide of the Ukrainian people, a stance that strongly contradicts Russia's denial of an artificial famine unique to Ukraine. But, these are only initial steps. Patriarch Kiril of the Russian Orthodox Church is seeking to limit the autonomy of the UOC-MP. On the other side, there are signals that the Ecumenical Patriarchate of Constantinople may recognize the autocephaly of the UOC-MP which will open the way for its unification with the UOC-KP.

President Yanukovych:
A Second Round of Regional Polarization

In the 2010 presidential elections Yanukovych's team mobilized around public disillusionment into the performance of Orange governments. His campaign also exploited slogans from the 2004 elections for mobilizing the regional electorate in the east and south of the country, including anti-NATO sentiments, promises to make Russian a second state language, and insistence that there was no falsified vote in 2004 when "our victory was stolen." Yanukovych even mentioned the possibility of recognizing the independence of South Ossetia and Abkhazia, a step totally in contrast with other Ukrainian presidents who made the territorial integrity of states a cardinal principle in Ukrainian politics.

As a result of this electoral rhetoric, the country was again polarized, this time by Yanukovych. In the second round in February 2010 Prime Minister Yulia Tymoshenko won in 16 regions and the capital, while Yanukovych won only in 9 regions and the city of Sevastopol. Despite his election promises to seek to overcome Ukraine's regional divisions his steps merely served to deepen them.

The April 2010 Kharkiv Accords with Russia permit the lease of the Russian naval base in Sevastopol for an additional 25 years (after the 1997 agreement expires in 2017) and prolong it after 2042 for another 5 years. This was signed even though it infringed the Ukrainian constitution, which declares there should be no foreign military troops on Ukrainian soil on a permanent basis. The decision was approved in parliament against the advice of three parliamentary committees and without necessary discussions, provoking a riot.

One of the most symbolic concessions to Russia was on the NATO question (see the chapter by Stephen Larrabee). Under Kuchma the position of the Party of Regions was quite conformist and in the *Strategy for Ukraine for 2004-2015* prepared under the auspices of then Prime Minister Yanukovych, the deadline for joining NATO was set at 2008. The Party of Regions unanimously voted in 2003 for the Law on the Fundamentals of National Security which clearly states that Ukraine's aim is to join NATO as well as a Memorandum with NATO to provide it with support in multinational exercises and peacekeeping operations. In 2006, during Yanukovych's second premiership, the Party of Regions supported the Memorandum with NATO on the participation of Ukraine's strategic transport aviation in NATO operations. This demonstrates that anti-NATO election campaigns by the Party of Regions were populist and designed to mobilize their electorate.

However, on July 2, 2010, the new law on Fundamentals of Domestic and Foreign Policy of Ukraine was adopted by parliament that proclaimed a non-bloc status for Ukraine aimed at establishing good relations with the Russian leadership. Yanukovych also played on the ambivalent geopolitical orientations of Ukrainians. According to a April 2010 poll by the Institute of Sociology, Ukrainian National Academy of Sciences, 62% were in favor of Ukraine joining the union of Russia and Belarus (negative attitude dominated only in Western Ukraine). The explanation is that this union is associated with cooper-

Table 2. How Do You Assess Ukraine's Entry to the European Union?

Percent

	West	Center	South	East	Ukraine
Rather negative	6.6	16.7	22.1	28.2	19.1
Difficult to answer	27.3	38.2	41.5	33.3	35.3
Rather positive	66.1	45.1	36.4	38.5	45.5

April 2010 poll of Institute of Sociology, Ukrainian National Academy of Sciences http://www.niss.gov.ua/articles/457/.

ation and visa-free travel. Simultaneously, as seen in Table 2, in all regions the number of those who support Ukraine's accession to the EU exceeds the number of opponents (the paradox is that the highest support was not under Yushchenko, but in 2000-2001 under Kuchma, when anti-Western campaigns has not yet been launched).

In the educational sphere Yanukovych also made concessions which helped Russia to strengthen its ideological influence in the region. In April 2010, during his visit to the Council of Europe in Strasburg, Yanukovych rejected the view that of the *holodomor* as genocide.[15] The appointment of Dmytro Tabachnyk as Minister of Education came after he was lobbied by Patriarch Kiril. His promotion served to polarize the country in the cultural-linguistic sphere as he is known for pejorative statements regarding the Ukrainian intelligentsia and for Soviet interpretations of Ukrainian history; for example, using the same Soviet allegations against the 1940s nationalist movement that they were "Nazis."

In contrast to all other Ukrainian presidents, who sought to strike a neutral balance between rival Orthodox Churches, Yanukovych has openly aligned himself with the UOC-MP. Symbolically, he received blessing in Kyiv from Russian Patriarch Kiril *before* he went to his inauguration in the Ukrainian parliament.

Parliamentary deputies from the Party of Regions submitted a draft law on languages in summer 2010 which would have upgraded Russian to the status of a 'regional language' throughout most of Ukrain-

---

[15]Parliaments of more than 20 countries, including the USA, Canada, Spain, Poland, Hungary, Argentina, Australia, Brazil, Baltic states and elsewhere have recognized the *holodomor* as a genocide.

ian territory. This would be a further blow to the Ukrainian language—as stated in the recommendations of the OSCE and the letter of OSCE High Commissioner on National Minorities Knut Vollebaek to Ukrainian Parliamentary Chairman Lytvyn.[16]

It seems that President Yanukovych made concessions on issues that are symbolically important to Russia but do not threaten his power. While playing on contradictions between different regions, the Yanukovych administration is seeking a monopolization of power over *all of* Ukraine and therefore would try to avoid threats of separatism or raising the issue of federalization. For example, Yanukovych's concessions to Russia on the Sevastopol naval base do not benefit local Crimean elites. Although Crimea's Prime Minister Vasyl Jarty is formally subordinated to the Crimean Parliament he and his entourage come from the town of Makeevka in the Donetsk region and *de facto* control the Crimean peninsula.

Many analysts have concluded that the Party of Regions is tacitly supporting the nationalist Svoboda (Freedom) party. In the October 2010 local elections Svoboda won in the three *oblasts* of Galicia. Their success coincided with the plans of the Party of Regions to destroy Tymoshenko and other radical opposition forces thereby opening up political space into which controlled, loyal nationalists such as Svoboda could be interjected.[17]

Conclusions and Recommendations

National integration, on the one hand, and democratic and market reforms, on the other, reinforce one other. National integration permits the introduction of painful reforms which are difficult to introduce in divided societies. At the same time, if reforms are successful, they provide the basis for national cohesion on other issues.

---

[16]These documents were released in www.RFE/RL.org, January 14, 2011. See http://docs.rferl.org/uk-UA/2011/01/14/original.pdf.

[17]See, for example, Mykola Pysarchuk and Olena Mihachova, "Partia 'Svoboda'—viddushyna dlia znevirenykh chy tekhnologia bahatorazovoho vykorystannia," *UNIAN*, January 20, 2011.

Despite the fact that the goal of European integration is not viewed by the majority of Ukrainians as a vehicle which could become a 'national idea,' the development of relations with the EU and integration into the EU is viewed positively in all regions of the country. Therefore, it is important that the average man and woman in the street, especially in the east and south of the country, would see benefits from these relations in the form of a visa-free regime, possibilities for younger Ukrainians to study abroad, the growth of cultural, educational, and professional exchanges, and learning from the European experience in providing local and regional self-government. The establishment of the Deep and Comprehensive Free Trade Agreement could provide additional 'carrots' for Ukrainian entrepreneurs to reform themselves and become more transparent in their business practices.

Information campaigns on NATO should highlight how NATO provides practical help to Ukraine in emergency situations, cyber-security, security to the Euro-2012 football championship, orders for Ukrainian industry, and support for the training of Ukrainian officers. NATO was for post-communist countries the stepping stone from which they joined the EU.

Legal changes at the national level should stimulate cooperation between regions and provide a framework for this endeavor. Constitutional reform should not be viewed as a zero-sum game and any reforms and establishment of a political system should have as an important objective the prevention of the monopolization of power. Instead of vacuous rhetoric about federalization, there should be real reform of local self-government which decreases the dependence of regions upon an all-powerful 'center.' Despite popular support for a return to a majoritarian electoral system (because it allegedly provides for a 'connection' between deputies, his district and voters), most analysts agree that the best way to support party development is to introduce open and regional party slates.

An Open Ukraine keen to introduce the radical reforms outlined in other chapters requires national integration and the overcoming of regional tensions that have become exasperated under Yushchenko and Yanukovych. It means that Ukraine should find a balance between support for the Ukrainian language and culture with respect for the rights of ethnic minorities. At the same time, the latter is impossible if Ukrainians continue to feel their culture and language is being subjected to discrimination. Therefore, the Ukrainian authorities should avoid policies that polarize the country, avoid the appointment of officials who are considered to be offensive to the majority of the Ukrainian population.

It is important to increase the role of civil society, for example, to involve competent experts in debating key appointments in the education sphere and in developing modern Ukrainian history textbooks. These textbooks should not be limited to the history of ethnic Ukrainians but be based on the standard Western frameworks of territorial, inclusive histories.

An Open Ukraine requires policies to develop modern Ukrainian culture, including popular culture. The biggest challenge for Ukrainian nation-building is to promote Ukrainian-language publications in the media, on talk shows, during popular performances, and through computer games. For example, it is important to keep a 50% quota on the radio for Ukrainian-language performances, in music and authors, and to develop clear criteria for what it means to support 'Ukrainian-language products.'[18]

For Western policymakers it is important to understand why the issue of keeping Ukrainian as the only state language is so sensitive to Ukrainians, why double citizenship is unacceptable and why they urge Russia, Hungary and Romania to respect Ukrainian laws regarding this issue. In general, Polish-Ukrainian reconciliation could serve as a model for relations between Ukraine and its neighbors.

In the sphere of inter-ethnic and inter-regional relations, an Open Ukraine requires policies that could be drawn from formulations drawn up by the Razumkov Center. These include:

- popularization of works by outstanding Ukrainian and foreign writers who advocated inter-ethnic tolerance and their inclusion in secondary school programs in literature;

---

[18]See the recommendations of the NGO expert consortium Ihor Burakovsky ed., *Nova vlada: vyklyky modernizatsii* (Kyiv: KISS, 2011), pp. 216-218.

- creation of a network of courses on the Ukrainian language for the adult population in Russian-speaking regions, including for specific target audiences such as civil servants, representatives of the judiciary and security forces;

- introduction of knowledge tests for civil servants of the state language and the language of communication of the overwhelming majority of local residents;

- inclusion of obligatory excursions, including to other regions, into school programs;

- implementation of a comprehensive national information campaign publicizing Ukraine's history and culture, the Ukrainian language, state symbols, and achievements of the country in different domains;

- familiarization of Ukrainian society (first of all, youth) with the history, culture, spiritual and household traditions of ethnic minorities;

- encouragement of inter-regional migration of youth to enter higher education;

- prevention of 'enclavization' of higher education due to the "approach to places of residence."[19]

Strong Western support remains important for the territorial integrity of Ukraine, in general, and for stabilization in the Crimea, in particular. To resolve the problems of deported ethnic groups, and first of all Crimean Tatars, it is important to adopt a law on the rights of these groups and in the socio-economic area to conduct an inventory of the land in the Crimea. The authorities should not attempt to split the Crimean Tatars and undermine the authority of the Mejlis; on the contrary, the role of consultative bodies of Crimean Tatars is to be increased. More Crimean Tatar youth should be provided with possibilities to study outside the Crimea, including abroad.

---

[19]See Common identity of the citizens of Ukraine, National Security and Defence, no. 9, 2007, pp. 28-31. Available at www.uceps.org/eng/files/category_journal/NSD93_eng.pdf.

A difficult question is how to make Sevastopol survive economically without a Russian naval base? This is part of a more general question of how to create a favorable investment climate in the Crimea, especially in tourism.

No preferences should be given to any religious confession. The question of the unity of divided Orthodox churches should be left to their own competence as the Ukrainian state can only support dialogue between them. The Ukrainian authorities should not be permitted to get away State Channel 1 devoting too much time to visits and statements by the Moscow patriarch: religious activity should be covered in media without its politicization. The role of the All-Ukrainian Council of Churches and religious organization should be increased, and draft laws regarding religious issues should be passed to the Ukrainian parliament *after* consultations with the council.

Chapter Three

Corruption, Rule of Law, and Ukraine

Bohdan Vitvitsky

This chapter is simultaneously addressed to two audiences: a Western one and a Ukrainian one. During my tenure in Ukraine, I often found that although many Ukrainians had learned and adopted terminology familiar in the West, they either had little understanding of what those terms and concepts meant or understood them in a way that was substantially different from the way in which they are understood in the West. In order to facilitate fruitful dialogue in the future, it is important to bridge those two conceptual worlds through conceptual elucidation. But even in the West, key notions such as rule of law are used far more frequently as platitudes than as clearly defined and understood concepts. Thus to advance discourse about corruption, rule of law and how high levels of the former and low levels of the latter relate to Ukraine, this chapter begins by offering a comprehensive conceptual framework for rule of law and corruption. It also introduces a distinction between episodic and systemic corruption, and it addresses Ukraine's post-Soviet "virtuality" problem. The chapter then discusses the current state of affairs in Ukraine as exemplified by the 2011 prosecutions of Yulia Tymoshenko and other former high government officials and discusses the Marxist-Leninist causes/sources of this state of affairs. It concludes with some suggestions and recommendations for reform in Ukraine and with some thoughts about an "Open Ukraine."

I begin with two propositions that are non-controversial.[1] First, as reflected in all recent surveys, it is undeniable that there are high lev-

---

[1] The views expressed in this paper are not necessarily those of either the U.S. Department of Justice or the U.S. Government but are simply those of the author.

els of corruption in Ukraine.[2] Second, high levels of corruption can and do infect a country's politics and significantly impede its economic development.[3]

Expanding upon these propositions further, let us ask why Ukrainians should care about whether there is a high level of corruption in Ukraine. The answer is that it is in their interest to care for several reasons. Most importantly, high levels of corruption can and do degrade the entire system of governance within a country, and they undermine the possibility of real, instead of make-believe, democracy. Second, high levels of corruption significantly distort a country's economy because, at a minimum, they create a large degree of uncertainty and allow for large-scale theft of money, property and other public assets. At a maximum, they can suffocate an entire economy through monopolization, confiscation and other practices.

But why should countries outside of Ukraine care about levels of corruption in Ukraine? Again, there are multiple reasons. First, there is the contagion problem. It is difficult to quarantine corruption within a given country. Because we live in an increasingly globalized economy and interconnected world, corruption in one country can easily spill over to its neighbors. For example, if contraband—whether consisting of drugs, weapons or humans trafficked illegally—needs to cross a border, customs or transport officials on both sides of the border will likely need to be corrupted.

Second, high levels of corruption can lead to a partially failed state, with all of the attendant headaches that such states can cause the international community. Third, the international community has spent

---

[2] See, e.g., the set of 61 surveys of corruption in Ukraine conducted in 2008-2009 by MSI for the Promoting Active Citizen Engagement in Combating Corruption in Ukraine Project. The surveys and accompanying analyses included national surveys, surveys by individual oblasts and surveys by sectors (e.g., corruption in the judicial system, in education, in connection with real estate transactions etc.). These surveys are available from Dr. Lyubov Palyvoda at palyvoda@ccc.kiev.ua. See the Freedom House evaluation of corruption at http://www.freedomhouse.org/images/File/nit/2011/NIT-2011-Ukraine.pdf; and the Transparency International survey of perceived corruption for 2010 at http://www.Transparency.org/policy_research/surveys_indices/cpi/2010/results.

[3] See the chapters in this volume by F. Stephen Larrabee and Serhiy Kudelia.

millions on helping countries such as Ukraine try to reduce corruption, improve their systems of governance and promote economic development. Presumably the international community has an ongoing interest in seeing returns on its investment for humanitarian, political and economic reasons.

What Is Corruption?

To speak constructively about corruption in a country such as Ukraine, that is, to say something more than that there is much corruption there and to bemoan that state of affairs, we need to do some prefatory work by establishing a key distinction about manifestations of corruption and also by explaining the relationships between corruption and rule of law. The working definition of corruption I propose is: corruption is an act or omission committed by a public servant who unlawfully and/or wrongfully uses his/her position to obtain some undeserved benefit for him/herself or his/her allies, contrary to duty and the rights of others. Before proceeding, let me explain what is meant by a public servant, a concept that I found to be foreign to some people in Ukraine. A "public servant" is anyone who works for the state; it is, thus, anyone whose salary is paid by the state. This includes the president, ministers, judges, policemen, custom agents and many others.

The most common forms of corruption are bribe-taking and exploiting conflicts of interest. By conflict of interest I mean a situation in which a public servant makes a decision, whether regarding hiring of personnel, procurement of goods or services for a government entity, or making a judicial or ministerial decision that is influenced by the financial, familial or partisan political interests of the individual public servant making that decision. Thus, to cite but a few examples, a judge who rules in favor of his political party in order to advance that party's interests or a minister who sells government property at a discount to his brother-in-law or the police official who buys computers for his police force from his wife's computer company are all guilty of a conflict of interest.

Systemic Corruption and Episodic Corruption

Corruption appears in all countries, and news of its occurrence can be found circulating around the world. This sometimes prompts people in countries such as Ukraine to say, "what's the big deal about corruption in Ukraine? Every country has corruption."

Yes, it's true that every country has corruption. But there is a fundamental difference between those countries in which corruption is systemic, and those in which it is merely episodic. Countries in which corruption is merely episodic demonstrate the following characteristics. When corruption occurs, the victims, or the witnesses to, that corruption have someone or some institution to which to report it, and they can do so with a reasonable expectation that, in most instances, that corruption will be investigated, stopped and its perpetrators punished. In such societies, the broadly and sincerely held belief is that corruption is not normal or acceptable behavior, and this belief is reflected in the laws, institutional arrangements and mechanisms adopted both to prevent corruption and to punish it when it is uncovered.

In countries in which corruption is systemic, its occurrence is widespread. There are no effective means of challenging it, that is to say, there are no institutions with the will and the authority to properly investigate and to punish those who engaged in corrupt acts. There are also no mechanisms in place to prevent corruption. And, the general societal assumption is that corruption is more or less normal, that it's just the way things are in the world.

A moment's reflection will probably persuade one that episodic and systemic corruption are polar opposites on an imaginary scale on which all countries can be placed. And there often are differences within a country as to location on the episodic/systemic corruption scale. For example, a country in which corruption can fairly be said to be episodic may nonetheless have a region or a city in which corruption is systemic.

When people speak about combating corruption, what they probably mean is that they want to help reduce a country's systemic corruption to merely episodic corruption. One more introductory point that needs to be made is that, thanks to the inventiveness of human ingenuity, combating corruption can itself be corrupted. This occurs when, for example, a government pursues its own partisan agenda of persecuting its opponents under the guise of supposedly combating corruption.

Corruption, Rule of Law, Economics and Culture

There are several relationships between corruption and rule of law, and they are very important. But before turning to that subject, it would be fruitful to note the importance of economic and cultural factors in any successful campaign to control corruption.

Public servants need to receive adequate salaries and benefits such as pensions in order to avoid the situation in which the authority or responsibility with which the public servant is charged is out of balance with that person's salary, benefits and working conditions. A policeman, customs official or judge who is paid a completely inadequate salary will be much more inclined to ignore his/her conscience and to sell his/her authority for a bribe or to engage in conflicts of interest to his/her benefit than is one who is adequately paid. This is so because if a public servant is adequately paid and can expect an adequate pension, that person is less likely to want to risk losing it all by engaging in corruption. As a practical matter, post-Soviet countries often have far too many public servants, and one of the first steps they need to take is to reduce those numbers in order to be able to pay adequate salaries to the smaller number of public servants.

With respect to cultural factors, what a society considers "normal" or "acceptable" behavior will have a profound influence upon what members of that society do or refuse to do, and this of course also applies to public servants. If bribe taking by judges is considered commonplace or inevitable, then it is much more likely that a new judge will have fewer reservations about taking his/her first bribe. If, on the other hand, bribe taking is considered by a society to be a shameful betrayal of public trust and of the oath of office that the judge swore upon becoming a judge, then it is much, much less likely that a new judge would even think about taking a bribe.

In addition to the impact of social norms upon the behavior of individual public servants, institutional pride and "esprit de corps" are also very important factors in the level of professionalism demonstrated by any particular category of public servant. Professional pride and professional integrity can be created and maintained by good leaders who demonstrate professional dedication to their particular institution, care about its reputation and care about the well being of the rank and file of that institution. Such leadership is perhaps most visible in the military of some countries, but it can also be created in any other institution, whether the police, the prosecution service or the health ministry.

Corruption and Rule of Law

In addition to societal attitudes about the unacceptability of corruption as well as institutional professionalism and *esprit de corps* being very important contributing factors to controlling corruption, a functional legal system is another very important factor. By a functional legal system I do not merely mean a system that has judges, police, prosecutors, lawyers and jails, but I mean a legal system characterized by rule of law, because, unfortunately, there are various legal systems with judges, police, prosecutors, lawyers and jails that are dysfunctional. To paraphrase a statement once made by the president of the Russian Republic, dysfunctional legal systems are those characterized by legal nihilism.

What Is Rule of Law and Why Is It Critically Important?

To start with the second question first, rule of law is critically important to the overall well being of any complex, modern society and it is very difficult to control corruption without it. Rule of law may be analogized to the spinal structure of a complex, modern society. If it develops straight and strong, then that society's economic, political and legal systems are likely to develop in a normal fashion. By normal fashion here I mean a market economy with proper regulation; a genuinely democratic political system; and a legal system that is committed to discovering facts, not inventing them, that provides balance between the rights of the accused and the authority of the government, and whose overall goal is justice, however imperfectly that may sometimes be achieved.

If the rule of law is weak, that is akin to a human skeletal structure being bent, deformed or stunted in its development; when that occurs, the entire body will be deformed. So it is with a society's economic and political structures. Without rule of law, a country is likely to be plagued by power hierarchicalism and/or the law of the jungle; by legal and/or political arbitrariness and, thus, economic unpredictability; and by social atomization and alienation from a society viewed as unfair and "other." By power hierarchicalism I mean a state of affairs in which the oligarch or dictator or commissar decides what right, benefit or punishment should be meted out to whom, and does so not on the basis of some neutral principles but on the basis of what is to that person's advantage or to the advantage of the group or system of which that person is a part.

Rule of law is also important for controlling corruption because without rule of law, it is very difficult to be able to formally enforce laws and rules intended to control corruption. Even in countries in which society expects its public servants to be honest and where the professional integrity of public servants is high, there still are public servants who are corrupt because of greed or lack of conscience. It is, therefore, necessary that every country have an effective enforcement system to investigate, prosecute and punish those public servants who have betrayed their public trust. A legal system with a low level of rule of law will not be capable of any effective enforcement.

What Are the Constituent Elements of Rule of Law?

I propose the following working definition of rule of law: it is a set of legal mechanisms and institutions that collectively produce what most citizens most of the time consider to be results that are just, in the sense of fair, and reasonable. Thus in a rule of law culture, citizens assume and expect that the legal system will provide justice. By contrast, in a culture in which rule of law is mostly absent, what can also be called a culture of legal nihilism, citizens assume and expect that the legal system has little to do with justice and is instead an instrument employed with few, if any, constraints by the more powerful in order to obtain further advantage by bureaucratic force.

In a complex, modern society, rule of law is maintained by and is the product of the *interaction* between a set of societal attitudes and expectations on the one hand, and the infrastructure of the rule of law on the other. By societal attitudes and expectations I mean, first, an understanding and appreciation on the part of society at large of the critical importance of rule of law as well as a commitment to its core principles. By core principles I mean a strong sense that the legal system must be *just*, which at a minimum means that every man/woman is equal before the law (as captured by the aphorism that "no man is above the law"); that the law should be applied *consistently*, rather than arbitrarily; and that those who apply the law must do so *impartially* (as captured by the aphorism that those who administer the law must play *by* the rules, not *with* the rules).

Second, by societal attitudes and expectations I also mean that there needs to be an *understanding* on the part of political, legal and journalistic elites of the infrastructure needed for rule of law as well as a *commitment* to its defense and preservation.

So, again, rule of law is the product of the *interaction* between, on the one hand, societal attitudes and the expectations of the kind I have just outlined, and the so-called infrastructure of rule of law on the other. What makes up this infrastructure? Two kinds of things: the technical components of rule of law and the institutional arrangements involved in implementing rule of law. By technical components I mean an appropriate constitution, laws and rules. By an appropriate constitution I mean one that can be and is taken seriously—one that, for example, does not contain multiple promises that everyone knows the government cannot possibly keep but *does* contain a clear statement of those that it can and must keep. By an appropriate constitution I also mean a constitution that accomplishes at least three key tasks. First, it needs to set out the separation of powers among branches of government as well as to clearly designate and circumscribe those powers. Second, it needs to identify an individual's rights vis-à-vis the state. And third, it needs to provide for its own orderly amendment.

A second technical component of the infrastructure of rule of law consists of laws that are adopted after notice and public debate, and that reflect the will of the majority without violating the constitutional rights of those in the minority. The third type of technical component of the infrastructure of rule of law consists of what those in the Anglo-American legal world call *due process rules*. These fundamental procedural rules require three things whenever the government intends to take any action against or affecting an individual, his rights or his property. First, the individual must receive adequate advance notice of the judicial or governmental action against him. Second, the individual must be provided a hearing before an *impartial tribunal* that will rule on the validity of the governmental action. Third, the individual and his counsel must be provided with a full and adequate opportunity to be heard at such a hearing.

But rule of law will not exist no matter how good the constitution, laws and rules may be if there is not an appropriate human element to implement them, and by appropriate human element I mean institutions such as a judicial system, a prosecution service, the police, an independent and active bar, and an independent legal academy. Most important among these is a judiciary that consists of judges who are professionally competent, independent, impartial and minimally corruptible. Rule of law also requires prosecutors and police who are professionally competent and minimally corruptible. Lastly, it also requires an independent bar and legal academy whose members are committed to the constitution, its primacy and to the defense of rule of law, and whose leadership is willing to defend rule of law publicly when it is being undermined.

Rule of Law in Ukraine and Selective Justice

The conviction and sentencing of former Prime Minister Yulia Tymoshenko on October 11, 2011, generated a firestorm of criticism. The European Union issued a stinging rebuke to Ukraine that same day by High Representative of the Union for Foreign Affairs and Security Policy Catherine Ashton.[4] The White House, the U.S. Congressional Helsinki Commission and a plethora of editorial pages in European and US media expressed similar criticisms. The Ukrainian

---

[4] "Declaration by the High Representative Catherine Ashton on behalf of the European Union on the verdict in the case of Ms. Yulia Tymoshenko," press release 364 at http://www.consilium.europa.eu/Newsroom.

American Bar Association aptly summarized the basis for the criticism as follows:

> The prosecution alleged the former Prime Minister had abused her authority in causing the state run energy company NAK Naftogaz to conclude an agreement with Russia for the supply of natural gas, an agreement which now is claimed to be financially disadvantageous for Ukraine. The agreement was executed openly and publicly debated at the time, and no fraud or collusion was ever alleged even during the Tymoshenko trial. The former Prime Minister's actions, therefore, constituted a political act involving another sovereign state. If the former Prime Minister exceeded her authority, the Ukrainian judicial system or Verkhovna Rada (Parliament) of Ukraine could have, and can still, act to void and repudiate the agreement. However, *ultra vires* acts, untainted by fraud, cannot be sustained as being criminal under any interpretation or view of the rule of law in any democratic society.[5]

But, the high profile conviction and sentencing of Tymoshenko should not obscure the even more profound and systemic problems with the Ukrainian legal system. Many of these problems were highlighted in an important report issued on August 12, 2011, prior to the Tymoshenko verdict and sentencing, by the Danish Helsinki Committee for Human Rights. The report is titled "Legal Monitoring in Ukraine II"[6] (hereafter "Legal Monitoring"). The specific subject of Legal Monitoring is the 2011 prosecutions of Tymoshenko and three other prominent members of the former Ukrainian government; namely, the former Minister of Interior Yuriy Lutsenko, the former First Deputy Minister of Justice Yevhen Koyniychuk and the former Deputy Minister of Defense Valeriy Ivashchenko. It is authored by a man who in addition to possessing extensive international experience

---

[5] "Statement of the Ukrainian American Bar Association on the Trial and Sentencing of Julia Tymoshenko," October 11, 2011, at http://www.uaba.org; "*ultra vires* acts" means acts that are beyond the scope of authority.

[6] The Danish Helsinki Committee for Human Rights, "Legal Monitoring in Ukraine II," available in English and Ukrainian at www.helsinki-komiteen.dk.

has also served as a Danish public prosecutor, as a chief of police and as deputy chief of the Danish Security Service. It is an outstanding report in the thoroughness and impartiality of its analysis.

More importantly for our purposes, Legal Monitoring is a scathing indictment of Ukraine's legal system from the perspective of what constitutes a civilized legal system in the 21st Century, regardless whether one is comparing Ukraine's legal system to a civil law or common law system.[7] Twenty years after Ukraine became independent, one finds that one after another of the procedures and practices employed today by the criminal justice system are patently unfair and, in some instances, extraordinarily so.

To cite but some of the examples discussed in Legal Monitoring, the young judge in the Tymoshenko case will in 3 years come before the Higher Council of Justice that will decide whether or not to reappoint him. Three prominent members of that Council are the Chief Prosecutor and two of his deputies, representing the same office that is prosecuting Tymoshenko before that same young judge. This is an obviously unacceptable conflict of interest to the detriment of the defendant.[8] Furthermore, incredibly—as this violates every precept of judicial independence—the Ukrainian Prosecutor General exercises a control function with respect to the judiciary. Thus, for example, in the last year the prosecution initiated 600 disciplinary cases against judges that resulted in 38 judges being dismissed, only a few of which cases had anything to do with criminality; in other words, only a few had anything to do with corruption.

---

[7] The term "civil law" system refers to any legal system that is a descendant of Roman, Justinian and later Napoleonic law; this is the system that can be found in various forms in continental Europe and South America. The common law system arose in England and is the system found today in England, the U.S., Canada and other present or former members of the British Commonwealth.

[8] Although the Council of Europe's Venice Commission emphasized that it was beyond its competence to take a position on the verdict in the Timoshenko case, on October 15, 2010, the Commission criticized the appointment of the judge charged with hearing the Timoshenko case on the grounds that as a temporary or probationary judge, i.e., as one whose reappointment was to be reviewed in 3 years, his independence could be questioned. "Venetsians'ka komisiya: spravu Timoshenko ne mozhna bulo viddavati Kireyevu," *Ukrayinska Pravda*, October 15, 2011.

The Lutsenko defense was not allowed to copy the case files containing thousands of pages of documents and was only given short periods of time within which to look at those documents. That is unacceptable in a rule of law system. It is also fundamentally unfair that under Ukrainian law the defense cannot appeal to a judge in order to force the prosecution to treat the defense fairly in such instances. Similarly, defense counsel for Tymoshenko was only given several days within which to prepare for trial in a case involving tens of volumes of documents. That is also unheard of in a rule of law system.

It is also unheard of in a rule of law system for a government to file criminal charges against high-ranking members of a former government where the gist of the allegations is that the defendants made political or economic decisions with which the current government disagrees. The same applies to questioning Tymoshenko on 42 separate occasions by the prosecutor's investigator; or jailing these defendants, none of whom is alleged to have committed a violent crime nor has a criminal record; or delaying medical care for Ivashchenko while in jail; or handcuffing defendants Lutsenko, Ivanshchenko, and Korniychuk and keeping them in a cage in court, and so on.

The Genesis of the State of Rule of Law in Ukraine and the Marxist-Leninist Destruction of Legal Justice

Because today's legal system in Ukraine is in most respects a continuation of the Soviet legal system, it is impossible to understand some of the bizarre legal practices and procedures going on in contemporary Ukraine without some familiarity with Soviet history and the Marxist theory that influenced its development. According to Marxist-Leninist theory, law as it existed in, for example, the West was part of the so-called "superstructure" of society. As such, so the theory went, law reflected and served the interests of the capitalist class rather than representing any general human ideal of justice or human rights. The law was, therefore, nothing more than a supposed instrument of the state in waging class war against the workers.

As recounted by the historian Richard Pipes, one of the first things that Lenin and the Communists did in December 1917 was to issue a "Decree on Courts" that did away with almost the entire then-existing legal system.[9] It did so by dissolving almost all of the courts and by doing away with the Procuracy, the legal profession and the justices of the peace. In its place Lenin's regime established Peoples' Courts as a substitute for local courts. The Peoples' Courts were intended to deal with crimes of citizens against citizens. More importantly, it also created so-called Revolutionary Tribunals to deal with people accused of "counter-revolutionary" crimes as well as speculation, looting and embezzlement.

Arbitrariness was a central feature of proceedings before these Tribunals insofar as they were charged with determining penalties while being, "'guided by the circumstances of the case and the dictates of revolutionary conscience.'"[10] As Pipes describes it, since *how* "the circumstances of the case" were to be determined and *what* constituted "revolutionary conscience" were left unexplained, the Tribunals operated as kangaroo courts and sentenced people to death or other punishment on the basis of the appearance of guilt. By 1920, procedural "bourgeois" holdovers such as the questioning of witnesses or the confrontation of defendant and plaintiff were discarded as overly burdensome and, the Tribunals' "judges" were selected by the Bolsheviks. The result was courts without laws to guide them, and a situation in which people were punished for crimes without the crimes having been given even semi-precise definition.

The system of "justice" was thus subjugated by Lenin to be wholly subservient to politics. And since there were no legally objective conceptions of right or wrong, or of guilt or innocence, there remained "only subjectively determined political expediency."[11] As the "law" was applied without the benefit of any formal legal guidelines, it ended up being interpreted very loosely, "as a political device serving the interests of the regime, whatever these happened to be at any given time."[12] As Pipes correctly described it, this was a world of legalized lawlessness.

---

[9] Richard Pipes, *Legalized Lawlessness: Soviet Revolutionary Justice* (London: Institute for European Defence & Strategic Studies, 1986).

[10] Pipes, op, cit., p. 9, quoting the January 1, 1918, instruction to such Tribunals issued by the Commissariat of Justice.

[11] Pipes, op, cit., p. 13.

[12] Pipes, op. cit., p. 14.

Once Lenin hijacked the legal system for the purpose of having it assist a totalitarian government control its population, there were no limits to how what passed for the "law" could be perverted. That is why the Soviet system staged show trials that more resembled the theatre of the absurd rather than any genuine legal proceeding, and that is why under Soviet leader Josef Stalin this system provided for fake legal proceedings that gave mass murder a make believe justification. The fake legal proceedings to which I am referring involved the so-called "troikas" of which the Soviet government made extensive use in the 1930's.

As recently described by the historian Timothy Snyder in his book *Bloodlands*,[13] the troikas were legal commissions used to implement state terror and mass murder. They consisted of a decision-making team of three persons: one member was the regional chief of the NKVD, one was the regional Communist Party chief, and one was the regional prosecutor. Prosecutors were ordered to ignore legal procedures. Confessions were elicited by torture. The three members of the troika would usually meet at night with investigating officers. They would hear a very brief report accompanied by a sentencing recommendation: either execution or the Gulag. The troikas handled hundreds of cases at a time *at the pace of sixty per hour.*

Why the Soviet government went to the trouble of organizing these farcical legal proceedings instead of simply killing the people it was going to kill or send to the Gulag anyway is an interesting question, but not one relevant to our discussion. The issues that *are* both relevant and important to our discussion are *that* such troikas were created and widely used and that prosecutors participated in them, as these facts exemplify the perversions in which the legal system was implicated.

During my anti-corruption work with the Ukrainian Parliament in 2009, I was told on one notable occasion that a major piece of anti-corruption legislation was not adopted because a prominent legal authority who had spent most of his life as a leader of the Soviet legal academy had declared that this legislation was inconsistent with "Ukrainian legal traditions." A Ukrainian colleague once told me that

---

[13] Timothy Snyder, *Bloodlands* (New York: Basic Books, 2010).

upon hearing such declarations he could not decide whether to laugh or to cry. But in some sense the prominent Ukrainian legal academic who made that statement was right. Given that the Ukrainian legal system is the direct descendent of the Soviet legal system, then it would *indeed* be inconsistent with that system to allow for anyone to try and make those in power accountable to the law or the people.

As is apparent from the Danish Report on Legal Monitoring, what has remained unchanged from Soviet times[14] is, first, the government's manipulation of the criminal justice system through its influence over the prosecution.[15] Secondly, its domination of the criminal justice system through, and by, the prosecution so that there is no impartial and independent arbiter standing between the prosecution and the defendant, a role that is performed in all rule of law systems by an independent judiciary. In rule of law systems, the prosecution is therefore accountable, as regards compliance with rules of fair procedure, to an independent judiciary. And furthermore, for example, in rule of law systems of the common law type, the prosecution's entire case is accountable to a jury of citizens that is held to be the "judges of the facts" and, thus, the ultimate judges of a defendant's guilt or innocence.

The continuities between what goes on in the legal world in Ukraine today and what Lenin and Bolsheviks initially wrought cannot be ignored. The law continues to be viewed as an instrument of partisan governmental power. That which is construed to be "illegal" is whatever the government in power finds to be politically expedient. And the various procedural safeguards that are at the heart of a rule of law legal system are absent or ignored. This state of affairs prompts the following conclusion. It is questionable whether a legal system

---

[14]Surprisingly, even Ukrainians with a democratic bent seem unaware that their legal system suffers the fatal flaw of being the direct descendant of the Soviet legal system. As I learned from conversations with individuals from all different political camps, the self-conception of Ukrainian lawyers regardless of their political or ideological inclinations is that the Ukrainian legal system is a "Roman" system, i.e., a civil law system, and that the *system* does not need to be changed. There seems to be little awareness that although the Soviet system had the appearance of a civil law system, it was fundamentally different from both civil and common law systems for the reasons described above.

[15]It didn't even occur to Ukraine's Chief current Prosecutor that he should not openly declare, as he has done, that he is a member of President Yanukovych's "team."

that was perverted to the point that, for example, prosecutors participated in pseudo-legal proceedings in which issues of guilt and death
sentences were decided within a minute or two that has not yet con-
fronted its past and has not yet cleansed itself of that terrible past can
now be expected to know how to create, maintain and fortify the rule
of law.[16]

"Virtuality," Reality and the Law

A functional legal system, one characterized by rule of law that
seeks justice, is also a legal system that seeks to establish what within a
court of law is true and what is false. This search for the truth, not
some metaphysical or mathematical truth, but truth in the sense of
believable facts, is of course necessary in the quest for justice. Rule of
law systems have a candid understanding that there is no infallible
process for the establishment of truth in the form of believable facts.
But rule of law systems go to great trouble and great lengths to try
and succeed at discovering the truth. That is why, for example, common law legal systems have extraordinarily elaborate rules of discov-
ery, evidence, cross examination and trial procedure developed and
refined over centuries. That is also why there are courts of appeal that
are required to explain in detail in their published written opinions for
all to see the justifications for their decisions to affirm or reverse
lower court rulings. It is these rules and procedures in the aggregate
that help these legal systems arrive at the truth in a large majority of
cases and situations.

Unfortunately, by contrast to rule of law systems, there is in
Ukraine, as is the case in most post-Soviet countries, a phenomenon I
will refer to as the "virtuality" problem. By this I mean the widespread

---

[16]In news items on August 24, 2011 (Ukraine's Independence Day) it was reported that
from jail Tymoshenko stated, among other things, that in five years the *real* criminals
will be in jail. Based on the contents of the Danish report, one can certainly understand Tymoshenko's frustrations with the numerous injustices to which she has been
subjected. Nonetheless, it is discouraging that instead of speaking about who is going
to put whom in jail, neither she nor anyone else in speaking about the need to fundamentally reform the Ukrainian legal system so that it begins to resemble a rule of law
system and so that every citizen of Ukraine can be assured that he or she will not be
abused and mistreated by it.

tolerance for making believe, for pretending that something is different from or even the opposite of what it actually is. Soviet legal history, with its political show trials, is filled with virtuality. The Soviets also sought to export this virtuality to the Nuremburg trials when their prosecutors sought to try and prove in court that the twenty-some thousand Polish officers murdered at Katyn and elsewhere were victims of the Nazis, whereas they had actually been murdered by the Soviet NKVD.

More recently in Ukraine, one can encounter the pretense that all prosecutions are independent and merit-based whereas there is good reason to believe that some are commenced at the direction of the government to camouflage a political vendetta. Or, for example, one can find that draft legislation intended to help curb corruption is then revised so as to make the legislation practically useless, and that this is done by none other than those who earnestly proclaim their devotion to combating corruption. As documented back in 2002 by Taras Kuzio, Ukraine's virtual struggle against corruption is a play that has, unfortunately, had a long run.[17]

That virtuality is not only tolerated but also accommodated in the Ukrainian legal system, has had catastrophic effects because in everyday affairs, the legal system must be, and in rule of law systems *is*, the last refuge of reality and truth. In connection with this it is noteworthy that historians have recently realized that, for example, in 16th and 17th century England, the process in courts of law for establishing facts and citizens' exposure to that process as jurors or court observers served to educate and sensitize the entire English population to the value and importance of ascertaining facts in everyday affairs.[18] Thus, the procedures and mechanisms created in law to ensure impartiality on the part of the judge and jury to the extent humanly possible and to ensure credibility in the information provided to the judge and jury were subsequently adopted and/or influenced the development of establishing facts in history, science and other human endeavors. These procedures and mechanisms reflected an emphasis on obtaining

---

[17]Taras Kuzio, "Ukraine's Virtual Struggle Against Corruption and Organized Crime," *RFL/RL Crime, Corruption and Terrorism Watch*, September 6, 2002.

[18]Barbara J. Shapiro, *A Culture of Fact; England 1550-1720* (Ithaca & London; Cornell, 2000).

and presenting testimony by impartial witnesses with first hand knowledge of the issues being examined and an emphasis on seeking corroborating evidence consisting of relevant documents or additional testimony. For a culture, such as Ukraine, in which virtuality continues to be a curse in public life, what might be thought of as the collateral ramifications of genuine legal reform could not be more welcome.

Although the virtuality problem extends far beyond the legal system,[19] our focus is on corruption and the legal system, so we need at least to understand that virtuality is a major impediment to real, rather than make believe, legal reform and combatting corruption. We also should understand that reformers need to be constantly vigilant against it. For example, the term "reform" has in Ukraine been virtualized and the Ukrainian word "reform" is translated into, and is supposed to have, an identical meaning to its counterpart in English. Every standard definition of "reform" interprets that term to signify a change that involves an improvement to or in something. Yet the term "reform" is routinely appropriated for all kinds of changes, whether by legislation, constitution or otherwise, that involve a change, but change without improvement. One needs, therefore, to avoid being duped by misuse of the term "reform."

What Needs To Be Done To Reduce Systemic Corruption To Episodic Corruption?

What Ukraine needs in order to reduce corruption is heightened societal awareness that corruption is a major impediment to economic development as well as a major impediment to full democratization and European integration. This awareness can be and needs to be spread by multiple social segments such as the business community, the portion of the legal community that services the business community, the media, religious institutions, universities, NGOs and others. But if everyone waits for someone else to do it, then it is not going to

---

[19]To the extent that post-Soviet virtuality has received attention, it has been in the context of political corruption. See, e.g., Andrew Wilson, *Virtual Politics—Faking Democracy in the Post-Soviet World* (New Haven and London: Yale, 2005) and T. Kuzio, "Political Culture and Democracy—Ukraine as an Immobile State," *East European Politics and Societies*, vol. 25, no. 88 (February 2011), pp. 88-113.

happen. Reform also obviously requires political leadership that is genuinely committed to reducing corruption. In some historical instances, leaders have responded to what a society demands—recall what has just recently happened in India where a hunger strike by an activist and citizens' outrage over corruption forced a reluctant parliament into action; in other instances far-sighted politicians have acted as true leaders by creating reform because they understood its long-term necessity.

In addition to helping the citizenry understand the great economic and political costs of corruption for the purpose of mobilizing public support for combating corruption, individuals and organizations interested in reducing corruption need to mobilize behind specific, concrete initiatives. For example, in 2009 two draft anti-corruption laws were introduced in the Ukrainian Parliament that were the products of two years of intensive work on the part of working groups of Ukrainian officials aided by international and local experts.[20] One draft law set out a detailed code of professional ethics for public servants that included specific rules relating to conflicts of interest. The other draft law set out in great detail the rules and design for an effective system of financial declarations by public servants. These two draft laws were evaluated by international experts to be, if they were to be adopted and properly implemented, among the very best in Europe. Such projects, and others like them, need to be actively discussed and debated in the Ukrainian media, in university classrooms, on talk shows and in various other public arenas. This is the only way that support for such reforms can be initiated and mobilized. Civil society must push for its adoption.

Lastly, Ukraine does not exist on an isolated planet far from any other society that has sought to reduce corruption. There is a wealth of international experience on how to reduce corruption, and Ukraine can and should take advantage of such experience. Ukraine can and should learn from the successes and failures of nearby countries, particularly from post-Soviet or post-socialist countries as Georgia, Poland and the three Baltic countries as well as from the successes and

---

[20]"Project Zakonu pro pravila profesiynoii etiki na publichni sluzhbi ta zapobihannia konflictu interesiw (4420-1)" and "Project Zakonu pro zachodi derzhawnoho finansovoho kontroliu publichnoyi sluzhbi (4472)."

failures of Western European and North American countries. But there is valuable experience to be gained from around the world. Albania introduced a model financial disclosure system. And one can learn from the long and difficult experience that Hong Kong and Singapore had in eliminating systemic corruption.

Establishing and Strengthening the Rule of Law

The level of corruption present in a society and the presence or absence of rule of law in that society are very closely connected in several different ways. In a modern, complex society, the absence of rule of law is legal corruption, and, furthermore, weak rule of law makes it very difficult to reduce any kind of corruption and make much sense to speak about corruption without also speaking about rule of law.

Ukraine, as do other post-Soviet states, needs to fundamentally and profoundly transform its legal system if it is to enjoy a rule of law system. As a practical matter, there is probably no other way of doing it than by coming to grips with the legal system's catastrophic Soviet past and the causes of that past. This needs to be done by studying that past from the perspective of analyzing to what extent that which happened was "just," in the sense of having been fair, and to what extent and how legal practices, procedures and institutions betrayed the core value of any rule of law legal system; namely, justice as fairness. Such analysis, combined with a genuine commitment to avoid the mistakes of the past, could then be used to reform the entire legal system, ranging from reform of the Legal Academy to reform of the laws, procedures and mechanisms that are a carryover from when the legal system was used to serve the purposes of a totalitarian government rather than to produce justice. Judges, thus, cannot be "accountable" to prosecutors, as was the case in the Soviet Union and remain the case in Ukraine today. Prosecutors should not be the partisan political arm of the government. Furthermore, anyone who is incapable of acknowledging the perversions of Soviet "legality" is not likely to be someone who is qualified to be a judge or to teach at a law school if Ukraine is to evolve to a state guided by the rule of law.

In common law systems, the rules governing the adversarial system keep everyone in line so that justice is undertaken in the majority of cases. Most often judges are appointed or elected after gaining many years of experience as prosecutors or defense lawyers. Once someone is charged with a crime, judges act like referees who rule on the fairness of whatever the prosecutor or defense lawyer seeks to do both before trial and during the trial. In civil law systems, magistrate judges who are part of an elite and independent judiciary perform many of the investigatory tasks that a prosecutor undertakes in common law systems, while trial judges play a much more active role in questioning witnesses and evaluating evidence. In such systems, prosecutors play a less important role than they do in common law systems. Justice is accomplished because an elite judiciary is highly professional, independent and impartial. Although this is a very complicated question, given the historical and cultural conditions prevailing in Ukraine, that the adoption of an adversarial system may be the more realistic method of establishing a rule of law legal system because it may not be feasible to expect to create a highly professional, independent and impartial judiciary on whom much of the system would be built from scratch.

So as to avoid the impression that problems with the legal system are somehow confined to the way criminal law is practiced, it is worth noting that practices that occur in Ukraine outside the criminal law are likewise unacceptable in a state governed by the rule of law. For example, it is unthinkable in a rule of law state for a squad of masked police special forces with machine guns to barge into a major law firm for purposes of rooting through that law firm's files at will, yet that is something that happened in Ukraine in 2010. It is also unthinkable for judges to be bribed to provide legal cover for patently illegitimate corporate raiding of businesses or "raiderstvo." This is when a criminal gang decides to expel the rightful owners of a business and sends a squad of masked gunmen to evict the rightful owners of that business while using as legal camouflage a court order granting the gunmen control of the business, is based on some fabricated legal basis and obtained from a corrupt judge.

Although, given its Soviet past, the changes that the Ukrainian legal system needs to undergo are systemic, specific concrete changes can and should be implemented immediately. To cite but one example, work on drafts of a new, reformed criminal procedure code has been going on for years with assistance from the European Union and North Americans. It is high time to adopt such a code and thus to help eliminate some of the worst abuses allowed by the current code that dates back to Soviet times.

Helping Ukraine Help Itself Reform

With regards Western assistance on reform of the rule of law and corruption in Ukraine the most important starting point is straight talk and tough love. Straight talk and tough love are somewhat inhibited by the dictates of diplomacy and by considerations of sovereignty, but an artful exercise of straight talk and tough love can overcome those inhibitions. U.S. Ambassador to Ukraine John F. Tefft gave a good speech at a public roundtable in Kyiv at which he spoke about how an independent judiciary and courts of appeals are central to protecting an individual from the state. As he explained:

> This is the essence of democracy and is the exact opposite of the way the judiciary and the legal system is used in authoritarian and totalitarian states where its purpose is to protect the state from individuals. Moreover, on a practical level, an independent judiciary promotes transparency by requiring the state to provide reasons and justification for its actions as it applies the law in particular cases.[21]

It would also be valuable for the West to develop a *long term* strategy to assist Ukraine to fundamentally reform its legal system and reduce systemic corruption. With respect to rule of law, there should be some serious consideration given to examining to what extent historical and cultural factors applicable to Ukraine's experience may resemble those that, for example, existed when the common law system was developed such as distrust of government. It would be also important to think about whether it might not make sense to recommend that Ukraine adopt certain features of the common law with respect to criminal procedure.

---

[21]Statement of U.S. Ambassador John F. Tefft at the Roundtable on the Role of Supreme Courts in Protecting Human Rights at the National Level, held at the Supreme Court of Ukraine, September 22, 2011; http://ukraine.usembassy.gov/supreme-courts.html.

As regards corruption, it is useful to keep in mind that it took Hong Kong and Singapore, the two best examples of countries that eliminated systemic corruption, about 20 years to achieve this objective. So persistence and patience are obviously necessary. It is, however, very noteworthy that Georgia has made significant strides to reduce corruption since the 2003 Rose Revolution.

It would also be useful for there to be coordination among Western countries and institutions in this endeavor. Furthermore, this endeavor should be focused on what is best for Ukraine rather than on what may be best for any given international organization involved in assisting Ukraine to undertake reforms. Finally, individuals from the West engaged in such endeavors must be knowledgeable both about legal systems and recent Ukrainian and Eastern European history. If an individual is unfamiliar with the nature of the Soviet system and the role that the Soviet legal system played within it, that person is unlikely to understand the legal culture in Ukraine or how to assist reforms. That person is unlikely to recognize manifestations of the virtuality problem and that person is unlikely to understand how to avoid overt and covert attempts to sabotage genuine anti-corruption efforts.

Open Societies, Trial and Error

In this chapter I have been critical about various aspects of the Ukrainian legal system and of Ukraine's high levels of corruption. It is, however, important to remind oneself that *all* societies make mistakes as all societies have people who are greedy and/or unprincipled and/or just stupid. But, rule of law develops and improves only *if* a society is capable of recognizing problems and also learning from its mistakes. Thus, English common law with its protections for the individual from the state can be said to have developed as an attempt to provide relief from the abuses of those in power. Much more recently, the U.S. introduced various reforms in the late 1970s in response to abuses of power of then President Richard Nixon carried out as part of the so-called Watergate scandal. For example, we greatly expanded the system of Offices of Inspector General so that every Department and agency has one. The mandate of Offices of Inspector General is to reduce fraud, waste, abuse and corruption in each Department or agency. Another reform the U.S. introduced was to make it illegal for the U.S. Internal Revenue Service (the Tax Service) to share anyone's tax or financial information with anyone else in government without a written order from a Federal judge. Even Federal prosecutors have to obtain judicial orders before he/she can obtain tax records in connection with a criminal investigation. This requirement was introduced because Nixon's team had ordered the Internal Revenue Service to provide it with tax and financial information relating to those whom they considered to be its political enemies.

Conclusions

In the face of a significant problem, such as Ukranie's high levels of corruption and weak rule of law, there are two possible strategies. One is to adopt the posture of an ostrich; that is, to hide one's head in the sand and to pretend that all is well. The other strategy is to acknowledge the existence of the problem, to confront it and develop policies to solve it. Central to the notion of an "Open Ukraine" is the idea of a society that is open to acknowledging everyday realities which means a society that is capable of realizing and recognizing its shortcomings. This means a society that is willing to view life as a process of trial and error in which we have the capacity to learn from past mistakes in order to create a better present and future. It is in this context that I urge Ukraine and that segment of the international community interested in its evolution to help it become an "Open Ukraine."

Chapter Four

Ukrainian Economy and Economic Reforms

Marcin Święcicki

The first section of this chapter analyzes the state of Ukrainian economic reforms following two decades of transition to a market economy. This analysis is followed by a summary of recent macroeconomic results and an overview of cooperation with IMF in combating the consequences of the global financial crisis. In the next section the business climate in Ukraine is investigated. The following sections analyze corporate legislation and trade in agricultural land, and compliance with WTO obligations as examples of how external actors can influence economic systems in transition economies. The crucial role of the Association Agreement and Deep and Comprehensive Free Trade Agreement between EU and Ukraine is discussed, and the chapter is rounded off with an investigation of the potential role of oligarchs. The chapter concludes with a set of policy recommendations.

Economic Reforms after Two Decades

After two decades of transition Ukraine is still far behind countries that joined the EU, including the three Baltic states, in economic reforms. According to the EBRD transition index Ukraine scores behind Georgia and Armenia in 4-5 dimensions out of nine and behind Mongolia in some of them (such as large scale privatization, and price liberalization).[1] The most advanced areas in Ukraine's transition to a market economy by 2010 were small scale privatization, price liberalization, and trade and the foreign exchange system. The least advanced were governance and enterprise restructuring, competition policy and infrastructure.[2]

---

[1] *Transition Report 2010* (London: EBRD, 2010), p. 4.

[2] Ibid.

The slow pace of economic reforms in Ukraine can be explained by the following factors. When the USSR disintegrated, unlike Central Europe, Ukraine faced a triple transition: building sovereign state structures; transforming the economy; and establishing democratic institutions. The Baltic states spent only 45 years under communism, whereas Ukraine was part of the USSR for almost 70 years. Unlike the Baltic states, Ukraine had no recent tradition of statehood and therefore no ability to revive pre-communist institutions.

Ukraine opted for a presidential, rather than parliamentary, system of power in the 1996 constitution, which was in effect until 2005, and to which it returned in 2010. The experience of 20 years of transformation proved that presidential systems in transition countries makes it more difficult to ensure the rule of law, checks and balances, an independent media and judiciary. All countries that have been successful in transformations in Central, Northern and Southern Europe adopted parliamentarian systems. Of course, the presidential system does not preclude the adoption of reforms. There are exceptions, such as President Mikheil Saakashvili, who has undertaken radical reforms in post Rose Revolution Georgia. A series of reforms were implemented by President Leonid Kuchma in the mid 1990s. Following the 2004 Orange Revolution, President Viktor Yushchenko missed the opportunity to introduce reforms in the first years of his presidential term when Ukraine had a presidential constitution. On the other hand, four years of parliamentary rule—2006-2010—were marked by weak majorities and personal conflicts between President Yushchenko and Prime Ministers Yulia Tymoshenko and Viktor Yanukovych.

Ukraine's successful accession to the WTO in May 2008, following 15 years of negotiations, was one of the very few achievements of this period in the area of economic reforms. President Yanukovych, elected in 2010, launched an ambitious plan of reforms in summer 2010, but implementation has been very slow due to a lack of political will, populist concessions ahead of parliamentary elections in 2012, and a deficit in government capacity to draft EU-compatible legislation.

An EU membership perspective was and remains the most powerful external factor contributing to successful transformations in post-communist Europe. In countries offered membership by the EU a great deal of new legislation was adopted and modern institutions were established. Ukraine has been denied a membership perspective by the EU, and among the former Soviet republics only the Baltic states were invited to join the EU. The Orange Revolution was a perfect opportunity for such an offer to be made to Ukraine when it would have led to discipline and provided direction for political leadership, experts and the general public. Denying a membership perspective was a historical mistake by the EU, as Gunter Verheugen observed after he had left the office of Vice President of the European Commission.[3] A Plan of Action between Ukraine and EU was adopted in 2005 and an EU-Ukraine Association Agenda approved in November 2009, but these were poor substitutes for membership, as they lacked sufficient technical support and disciplining measures.

Macroeconomic Balances

Following a 15 percent GDP decline in 2009, the Ukrainian economy grew 4.2 percent in 2010 and is expected to grow by 4.5% in 2011 and 5.0% in 2012. By 2012 Ukraine's GDP will exceed its pre-crisis level. Economic growth is led by consumption that declined by 12.2% in 2009 and is expected to recover by 4-5% per year. Investment in fixed assets were slashed by half in 2009 and are recovering at a similar speed. The CPI is expected to grow by 11.4% in 2011 after it remained down by 9.1% in 2010.

In 2009 exports declined by 22% whereas imports were slashed by almost 40%. Both recovered in 2010 and 2011. Ukraine's current account deficit declined from 7.0% of GDP in 2008 to 1.5% of GDP in 2009. However, the World Bank expects the current account deficit to increase to 4% in 2011 and 5% in 2012 and 2013. FDI declined from $10.9 billion in 2008 to $4.8 billion in 2009 and remained low in 2010 and 2011. Nevertheless a surplus in FDI has compensated for the deficit in Ukraine's current account.

In 2011 proceeds from the privatization of Ukrtelecom and successful Eurobond placement contributed to an increase in the foreign reserves of the National Bank. The external debt is to decline from 91% of GDP in 2009 to 78% in 2011. While the indebtedness of

---

[3] For example, during the Economic Forum in Kyiv in February 2011.

companies and business persons is declining as a share of public debt while government debt is growing. Ukraine's public debt has been growing rapidly during the crisis from the low level of 12.4% of GDP in 2007. The World Bank predicts that public and guaranteed debt of Ukraine will grow to 40% of GDP in 2011 and will stay at this level for a couple of years requiring fiscal discipline and substantial reforms envisaged in the 2010 Standby Agreement with the IMF.

International reserves declined from $38 billion in August 2008 to $24 billion in April 2009 but have been recovering since then. Devaluation of the *hryvna* from 5 to 8 *hryvna* per U.S. dollar during the last quarter of 2008 had a positive impact on reducing the foreign trade deficit and contributed to the arrest of the depletion of Ukraine's currency reserves.

Ukraine's future fiscal balance is heavily dependent upon two reforms: energy tariffs (including gas prices for household consumers) and pension reform. Both are part of the IMF Standby Arrangement with Ukraine. In 2010-2011, Ukraine introduced the first stage of tariff reforms by raising household utility prices by 50% but balked at doing this a second time. Pension reform was adopted by parliament in summer 2011.

Cooperation with the IMF

Ukraine signed a Standby Arrangement (SBA) in an early phase of the global financial crisis in November 2008. However, in the course of the 2010 presidential election campaign Ukraine did not implement reforms aimed at lowering fiscal deficit, in particular reforms in the pension system and household tariffs. In October 2009 a new Social Standards Law was adopted by parliament that resulted in "significant budget pressures due to indexation of wages and pensions to the minimum wage and subsistence levels".[4] In July 2010 a new SBA was approved with the IMF worth $16 billion, available to Ukraine over 2.5 years, conditioned by reforms in its financial sector. The SBA entailed a new approach, the so-called "Exceptional Access Criteria," which allows for increased amounts of the loan for a member country

---

[4] IMF Country Report No. 10/262 (August 2010).

that is experiencing "exceptional balance of payment pressures" but at the same time having the "political capacity" to deliver sustainable adjustment measures in the medium term. Structural reforms are to bring the budget deficit down to 3.5% of GDP in 2011 and 2.5% of GDP by 2012.

The agreement with the IMF assumes a wide range of reforms aimed at improving the financial sector, in particular through the rehabilitation of the banking sector, improved tax collection, strengthening independence of the National Bank, and an increase in exchange rate flexibility. But reforms to the pension system and energy sector are critically important for restoring Ukraine's financial sustainability.

Pension expenditures increased from 9% of GDP in 2003 to 18% in 2009, one of the highest levels in the world. At the same time, pension fund revenues cover only two-thirds of expenditures, the rest being covered by transfers from the budget. Demographic pressures will increase the burden on the working population even further. The reform of Ukraine's pension system has been long delayed until summer 2011. The new law provides for raising the pension age for women from 55 to 60 years over 10 years by half a year per annum; raising the pension age for male civil servants from 60 to 62 years, increasing the qualification period for pensions from 25 to 30 years for women and from 25 to 35 years for men, lifting the minimum insurance period from 5 to 15 years and capping maximum pension benefits for new pensioners to 10 "living wages" (currently 7,600 *hryvni*, or about $950) The transition from the pay-as-you-go system to a capital accounts system is delayed until the budget of the pension fund and general budget are balanced.

According to the EU/UNDP BRAAC report, only a gradual increase of the retirement age to 65 years for both genders by 2050 would prevent a dangerous increase in demands placed on the pension system.[5] If the pension age remained unchanged, 55 for women and 60 for men, the Ukrainian population of pension age would increase from 11.7 million in 2009 to 14 million in 2050, whereas the working-age population would decrease from 27 to 17 million.

---

[5] *Demographic and Financial Preconditions of Pension Reform in Ukraine: Forecast 2050* (Kyiv: EU/UNDP Blue Ribbon Analytical and Advisory Centre, 2010), pp. 8-9.

Ukraine is one of the least energy-efficient countries, consuming 2.6 times more energy per GDP unit than on average in OECD countries. Industrial prices for energy are already at market levels. But prices for gas for households and utilities are heavily subsidized, and owners of large apartments and dachas are the greatest beneficiaries of low domestic prices for gas. With low gas prices there is neither the stimulus nor ability to invest in increasing the domestic extraction of gas. Therefore, Ukraine's domestic extraction of gas is "well below potential."[6] The only beneficiary of the artificially increased demand for gas are foreign suppliers, in particular the Russian state gas company Gazprom. In contrast, the Ukrainian state gas company Naftohas needs budgetary support.

According to the IMF SBA, Naftohaz's deficit is to be eliminated, beginning in 2011. The SBA provides for strengthening the social safety net for the poorest segments of the population as household utility prices are increased, with domestic gas prices being brought into parity with import gas prices. The first increase of household utility prices by 50% was implemented in September 2010. However, the next 50% increase, planned for April 1, 2011, was not introduced, due to the upcoming 2012 parliamentary elections.

Following two tranches (2.250 billion SDR), further installments of the SBA are suspended because prospects for sustainable finances remain uncertain. The third tranche was to be provided following a second review in March 2011. Yet an IMF mission to Kyiv to continue discussions on the second review of the SBA in October 2011 did not produce a breakthrough.

Business Climate[7]

The new Nikolai Azarov government (March 2010-) gave its commitment to deregulation but has prioritized big industrial business. Small and medium businesses feel neglected and are afraid of a further toughening of the administration of taxes.

---

[6] Ukraine—Request for Stand-By Arrangement, IMF Country Report No. 10/262 (August 2010) p. 12.

[7] This subchapter draws upon the study by Volodymyr Dubrovskiy prepared for BRAAC in March 2011.

Administrative reform has led to elimination of the SCURPE - an institution playing the role of "Ombudsman" for small businesses. Its functions were transferred to the Ministry of Economic Development and Trade (former the Ministry of Economy), creating an obvious conflict of interests.

Business registration is not a big issue, compared to other barriers.[8] According to the *Doing Business 2012*,[9] Ukraine was ranked 112 among 183 countries in the field of ease of registration procedures, and had overall rating of 152, a decline by 3 positions in comparison to the 2011 Report.[10] These conditions are worse than in OECD countries (especially, in terms of length and number of procedures, as registration in Ukraine takes almost twice as long and requires almost twice as many procedures), and even in comparison to Eastern Europe and Central Asia. The minimal capital requirement for a limited liability company was decreased to one minimal monthly wage (about $100),[11] which has made Ukraine look better in international comparisons.

According to the Law on State Registration, the entire procedure of registration in the State Tax Administration, State Pension Fund and State Statistics Committee should go through the "one-stop shop." But, in reality it works in such a manner only in the city of Vinnitsa and partly in a few other towns. The problem is that the law allows for other opportunities too, and applicants are compelled to use them.

Although registration is definitely not a bottleneck in business development and should not be prioritized at this moment, there is a lot of room for improvement. Closing a business is more cumbersome. In the *Doing Business 2012*, the country's rating on this position is 156.

---

[8] The respective question was last asked in a survey in 2004, (http://www.ifc.org/ifcext/uspp.nsf/AttachmentsByTitle/IFC_Ukraine_BE_Survey_2005_Eng/$FILE/IFC_Ukraine_BE_Survey_2005_Eng.pdf). At that time only 44% of respondents considered registration as as a significant impediment to their business compared to 54% a year before, while 66% complained about taxation. Registration does not seem to be a big issue for small and medium enterprises.

[9] *Doing Business 2012* (Washingon DC: World Bank, October 18, 2011).

[10]http://doingbusiness.org/data/exploreeconomies/ukraine#starting-a-business.

[11]Law No. 1759-VI of December 15, 2009 "On the Legal Amendments Concerning Simplification of the Business Conditions in Ukraine."

Licensing[12] *and permits*[13] are much greater issues for SMEs than registration. According to the IFC (2005)[14] they were rated third after taxation and cross-board trading. In this category Ukraine was ranked as 179 in *Doing Business 2011* and 180 in *Doing Business 2012*.[15] The total cost (as a percentage of per capita GDP) for obtaining a typical set of construction permits is almost three times higher than the region's average, and more than ten times higher than in OECD countries. Completion of the process of obtaining these permits requires much more time as well: 374 days compared to 166 on average in the OECD. The situation with construction permits is just an example that reflects the overall problem of registration. In the *Doing Business 2012* rating for Ukraine there is a further decline by three positions to 182.

The "silent is consent" principle was introduced by the Law on Amendments of Some Laws of Ukraine regarding Simplification of Business Conditions in Ukraine (No. 1759-VI of December 15, 2009) but it still does not work because another law stipulates a penalty for undertaking business activity without a permit. This contradiction is expected to be resolved by another bill (No. 6339[16]).

The same law introduced the most substantial improvement in the field of licensing as, unlike before, most licenses are now in perpetuity. By the government's own admission,[17] in 2010 it cancelled licensing of 90.2% (2046 out of 2268) kinds of businesses, and 27% (23 out of 78) kinds of activities. The simplification mainly boils down to aggregation of the licenses; for example, instead of licensing of each particular kind of construction work, like plaster, the entire complex is covered by a single license. This is, of course, a simplification of the paperwork

---

[12] A license is official permission to perform certain types of economic activity (for instance, sell alcohol).

[13] Permit is a general name for documents certifying that certain conditions are met and therefore a certain type of economic activity can be performed (for instance, a permit is required to start construction or use certain types of machinery).

[14] *Business Environment in Ukraine, 2005.* Ukraine Business Enabling Environment Project's report (Washington DC: The International Finance Corporation (IFC), 2005).

[15] *Doing Business 2012*, op. cit.

[16] http://w1.c1.rada.gov.ua/pls/zweb_n/webproc4_1?id=&pf3511=37592.

[17] http://www.dkrp.gov.ua/control/uk/publish/printable_article?art_id=171378.

but not a genuine deregulation. Also, there are widespread apprehensions that the new Town Planning Code makes developers' life easier at the expense of the interests of local communities, the environment, and architectural issues.

All in all, deregulation was undertaken mostly in respect to licenses[18] and permits that were in relatively short demand. As a result, despite an impressively long list of cancelled licensing procedures,[19] these cover just a few per cent of the total number of licenses that businesses should obtain. The most substantial improvements are in the cancellation of licensing for tourist agencies (but not operators), custom brokers, fitness and health-improvement. Nevertheless, the real situation with permits remains unclear as there is no register of them.

Standardization and certification procedures inherited from the Soviet command economy were burdensome and anti-innovative, imposing precise requirements regarding materials, components, and procedures of production. All industrial sectors had to produce the same few sort of sausages or shoes that were precisely described by the GOST-state agency, which determined standards. The safety of consumers was not specifically described but was assumed to be guaranteed by precisely required components and technologies.

Only in December 2010 did parliament approve two key laws, one on state market surveillance of non-food products and the other on basic safety of non-food products. These provide for the introduction of EU principles and procedures of market surveillance. The main idea of the EU system is to focus on safety features for consumers, regardless of what components and procedures are used in production. Introduction of the EU system requires—as was the case in all former Soviet bloc countries that joined the EU—enormous work in adopting EU safety directives and building new institutions, and in terms of acquiring the human capacity required for market surveillance. There are some laboratories and competent staff in Ukraine that could be employed with the new model, but only after extensive training and following institutional and technical adjustments. Besides, these new

---

[18]Law No. 2608-VI of October 19, 2010.

[19]For example, http://ukr.lcg.net.ua/licences/cancelled/.

laws do not apply to foodstuffs, which is the main and most problematic type of goods.

Taxation is certainly the main problem in Ukraine's business climate. In the *Doing Business Paying Taxes* 2011 and 2012 rating Ukraine is given the 181th position, the lowest among all country ratings, and the third from the bottom. The December 2010 Tax Code provides for:

- gradual reduction of rates of corporate income tax from 25-16% by 2014;

- reduction in VAT rates from 20-17% by 2014;

- reduction in some fines.

The vast majority of business entities are sole proprietors who normally use the simplified taxation system, which entails fewer costs in accounting and compliance, and attracts fewer inspections.[20] Sole proprietors were allowed to pay a unified lump-sum tax of up to –200 *hryvni* monthly, according to Presidential Decree No. 727/98 of July 3,1998. Revenues were shared between the state (local) budget and the Pension Fund. Businesses using the simplified taxation were exempted from full bookkeeping.

The new Tax Code reforms the simplified taxation in five major ways:

a. major increase in lump sum tax for sole proprietors. The tax was frozen at 200 *hryvni* since its inception in 1998 despite the multiple growth of CPI and salaries. Since the implementation of the unified tax, average salaries have grown more than 20 times and the CPI has increased more than 5 times. Nevertheless, the abrupt increase in lump sum tax has eliminated many small companies.

b. introduction of monthly, instead of quarterly, reporting based on books that in practice eliminated substantial simplifications for sole proprietors.

---

[20] *Investment Climate in Ukraine as Seen by Private Businesses.* Ukraine Business Enabling Environment Project Report (Washington DC: The International Finance Corporation (IFC), 2009).

c. introduction of "special factual inspection' that, in fact, nullifies restrictions on the number and time length of inspections in some sectors.

d. demanding bookkeeping be based on primary documents.

e. exclusion of payments to sole proprietors using simplified taxation from business costs, making such contracts prohibitively expensive.

VAT refunds remain a major problem, as they are being paid back initially to well-connected firms, with the remainder waiting for refunds for years. The Code stipulates so-called "automatic" VAT reimbursement, although only for firms meeting very strict conditions.

Changes in the rates should be introduced steadily in order to allow businesses to become adjusted to them. They should be also supported by the lowering of non-tax barriers. Hundreds of thousands, if not millions, of people working in businesses because taxes were so low have moved into the shadow economy or become unemployed.

The new Law on a Single Social Contribution (No. 2464-VI of July 8,2010) has merged a number of minor payroll taxes with the main one (contributing towards the Pension Fund) and delegated the administration of this tax to the State Pension Fund. This law simplifies payments and reduces inspections for companies using the basic system of taxation and unified tax payers who have employees (on which they have to pay the payroll tax). In the meantime, it complicates tax compliance and effectively increases the rate more than two times for sole proprietors who are paying a unified tax. In addition to single quarterly payments of the unified tax, they now have to make another one that exceeds by half the upper level of the unified tax rate. Although the 2010 tax code has partly reduced the complexity of paying taxes, the code did not address the main problem of mandatory contributions and payroll tax which remains set at a very high rate. Here reforms would need to be more radical.

The 2010 Tax Code is a controversial document because it introduces some positive amendments, especially for large business and some negative, mainly for small and medium businesses. The Tax Code partly simplifies the structure of tax legislation by converging it into a single law. The Code allows the "administrative" (hence, without a court's sanction) arrest of a taxpayer's property for 72 hours, which in many cases is sufficient for inflicting unacceptable losses to businesses, especially to SMEs that are generally more financially and legally vulnerable than larger companies. Third, it introduces a requirement for monthly reporting on personal income tax. The attempt to drastically increase tax rates of simplified taxation for sole proprietors was reduced by massive protests of entrepreneurs in Fall 2010 (the so-called Tax Maidan).

Improvements in transparency and accountability should be accomplished by the new Law on State Procurement, adopted on January 28, 2011. More competitive procedures should help mid-size companies and, in some cases, larger business entities. However, the law in practice would not allow small- and medium-sized businesses to participate in public procurement.

The burden of regulations related to export (and import) activities is also very high. In addition to VAT reimbursement, the Doing Business rates in "Trading Across the Border" rank Ukraine 139th, which is better than the country's overall rating, but much worse than for OECD countries. This is mainly due to custom clearance times that are estimated at 31 days for exports and 36 days for imports—almost 3 times more than the OECD average. The 2010 Tax Code attempted to forbid any kind of foreign trade activities for sole proprietors using simplified taxation arguing that some of them do not pay VAT on imports and import duties—which are not valid for exporters.

Ukrainian corporate legislation[21] is considerably underdeveloped in comparison not only to EU member states, but even to such countries as the Russian Federation, Kazakhstan or Mongolia.

The Economic Code. The distinctive feature of Ukrainian corporate legislation is preservation of out-dated Soviet-era concepts that leave unclear divisions of property rights and management functions. The Economic Code of Ukraine, the law on enterprises in Ukraine and the law on management of state property objects permit daily administrative interference in management of state enterprises, maintain the primacy of the state over private property, and confuse owners' and man-

---

[21]This subchapter draws upon the study by Anatoliy Yefymenko prepared for BRAAC in 2009-2011.

agement decisions. Uncertainty over the legal status of property of "economic entities" leads to corruption (especially in state-owned enterprises), avoids responsibility for breach of legal obligations and provokes unfair behaviour by parties, thereby undermining stability of property ownership and hindering of the development of economic growth due to a high risk of non-payment. Until the Economic Code is abolished, progress in the development of corporate legislation and improvement of regulation in other spheres will be difficult to achieve. Therefore, for an "Open Ukraine" to become the future of Ukraine, the Economic Code should be abolished.

The Civil Code of Ukraine (CCU). Provisions in the CCU on regulation of legal entities are mostly consistent with legal approaches common to all European countries. A few provisions contain mistakes that create unjustified risks and undermine efficiency of regulation (e.g. provisions on artificial requirements on maintaining a ratio between net asset value and charter capital for joint-stock and limited liability companies). These should be brought into conformity with the requirements of the Second EU Company Law Directive.

Law of Ukraine on Joint-Stock Companies. In September 2008, Ukraine adopted a law on joint-stock companies which was an important step in moving Ukraine closer to modern corporate law standards. However, the law preserved the out-dated "the winner takes all" principle, according to which the controlling shareholder has the possibility to subdue the joint-stock company's activities to his or her interests. Minority shareholders are regarded as a source of problems, such as difficulties reaching quorum and useless expenses (i.e. burdensome notification requirements). The situation is aggravated by the fact that the capital of most Ukrainian joint-stock companies is excessively concentrated and the minority shareholders' stake does not allow them to influence the company's policy.

However, Ukrainian joint-stock companies will not be able to attract substantial investments without realizing that nobody will invest without guarantees of their participation in profit-sharing and decision-making. Minority shareholders should be provided with powerful enough instruments allowing them to protect their interests in a reliable manner. According to the World Bank *Doing Business 2012*, Ukraine poorly protects investors, not providing even half of the protection level of, say, New Zealand.[22] The corporation's legal model under the Ukrainian law on joint-stock companies vests the controlling shareholder with powers of unrestricted domination in company management and tools to misappropriate all the company's profits, factors that reduce incentives for investors.

Building investors' confidence in Ukrainian joint-stock companies requires revision of legal concepts of the law on joint-stock companies and substantial amendments to the text of law. For Ukrainian joint-stock companies to be able to perform the function of capital accumulation (through raising investments) in an efficient manner, it is necessary to replace the "winner takes it all" with an "investor friendly" model, which would allow minority shareholders to feel secure.

Limited Liability Companies. Limited liability companies are the most common organizational and legal form for small and medium-sized business. More than 400,000 limited liability companies are registered in Ukraine, and their share in GDP output shows a steady growing trend. However, the quality of legal regulation of limited liability companies remains unsatisfactory thereby reducing the capacity of these organizations.

Legislation on limited liability companies suffers from numerous deficiencies that unnecessarily restrict the flexibility of this form of corporation,[23] and fails to secure effective protection of minority shareholders' rights. Limited liability companies regulating legislation also reproduces the "winner takes it all" model that does not allow Ukrainian limited liability companies to efficiently perform the function of the pooling of capital and turning relations among company members into a bitter struggle for control over the company's executive body and its cash flows. Moreover, legal tools to control managers remain too weak leading to unnecessary and often inefficient concentration of ownership, thereby complicating the separation of management from ownership. This makes the attraction of additional investors risky and unattractive and brings a number of other adverse consequences. Therefore, there is a need for a new law that would

---

[22]*Doing Business 2012*, op cit., p. 12.

[23]http://brc.undp.org.ua/img/publications/TOB%20-LLC%20law%20ENG(23)%20(1).ppt.

resolve these and other problems that are hampering the development of limited liability companies.

The lack of proper regulation of limited liability companies hinders direct foreign investment in Ukraine. Foreign investors do not wish to engage Ukrainian partners or managers due to high risks of corporate raiding or loss of investment arising from conflict between company members. The draft Law on limited liability companies is an interpretation of the Russian law and continues to include the shortcomings found in the law of Ukraine on business associations.

Regulation of Insolvency and Bankruptcy. Ukraine ranks 156th among 183 countries in the world in the "closing business" indicator. The average duration of bankruptcy procedures in Ukraine is 2.9 years, the costs of bankruptcy proceedings reach as high as 42% of the debtor's property value on average, whereas the collection rate is at most 7.9% of the value of creditors' claims.

Under these current conditions, the law of Ukraine on re-establishing solvency of a debtor or declaring a debtor bankrupt encourages unscrupulous conduct and provides grounds for illegal enrichment. This is undertaken through companies escaping compliance with commitments or through seizure of somebody else's assets, two factors that adversely affects the macroeconomic situation in Ukraine and results in degradation of its industrial base and human capital. Legal concepts dealing with regulation of insolvency and bankruptcy towards identification and respect of personal interests of all parties involved should be revised. There needs to be introduced sound motivation of a bankruptcy commissioner through a combination of legal tools for control over his decisions, fair compensation for performance and liability for losses.

Establishment of an Agricultural Land Market. Land reform, which has been implemented in Ukraine since 1991, has not created a fully-fledged market for agricultural land. Most of Ukraine's agricultural land is parcelled into 6.7 million plots of only 1.5 to 15 hectares The average size of land holdings is approximately 4 hectares. Trade in farmer's land certificates began in Ukraine in 1994, but without the adoption of proper legislation that would have resolved the transfer of land certificates.

A temporary moratorium on the sale of agricultural land was introduced on January 1, 2002. This moratorium has been extended several times since then and is still in effect today. The moratorium does not restrict the exchange of land holdings through family succession, as a gift or in the form of an exchange.

The leasing of land is the main way of transferring land due to the effective moratorium on sale of agricultural land. Lease agreements are typically being concluded for a term of 4 to 5 years (accounting for almost 50% of all lease agreements). The moratorium on trade in agricultural land is to be lifted provided legislation is adopted that would regulate the land market and cadastral system. The law of Ukraine on the land market (developed by the State Agency for Land Resource of Ukraine) was adopted in summer 2011 and proposed to establish a special state institution for managing state owned lands that are cultivated for agricultural purposes.

This specialized institution is responsible for:

- ensuring implementation of state policy on regulation of the cultivated land market and for state policy of preserving and enhancing the state fund of agricultural lands;

- consolidating agricultural land;

- resolving problems associated with ownership rights of deceased private land holders;

- realizing the right to the primary acquisition of agricultural land shareholdings on behalf of the state in the event of their sale;

- issuing mortgage securities;

- carrying out activities related to the planning of land use and control over and protecting agricultural lands.

The law on the land market does not permit foreign individuals or companies to own agricultural land. The adoption of the further legislation is envisaged to open up trade in agricultural land on the State Land Cadastre, on Consolidation of Lands, and on a Land Inventory.

Compliance with WTO commitments.[24] Ukraine became the 152th WTO member in May 2008, following 15 years of negotiations. In the years preceding WTO accession Ukraine adopted or revised 55 laws to comply with WTO rules within the 5 year transition period granted to Ukraine to fully comply with its commitments.

Ukraine undertook steps in order to adjust its system of foreign trade to meet WTO commitments. External tariffs were transformed into ad valorem and rates are to be set in accordance with Ukrainian commitments. Quantitative restrictions are to be abandoned. Ukraine is committed to decrease export duties and refrain from applying any obligatory minimum export prices. Sanitary measures are to be applied according to WTO requirements.

Subsidies, in particular in the agricultural sector, are to be gradually reformed in order to reduce measures falling into the "amber box" and develop the "green box" of instruments. Domestic support for agriculture under the "amber box" in 2009 did not exceed the Aggregate Measure Support permitted by the WTO.

Development and implementation of new "green box" programs should become a fundamental direction of state policy on agricultural support following Ukraine's accession to the WTO. The WTO does not impose any restrictions on the amount of state financing for "green box" measures. Around 95% of the budget funds under Ukraine's "green box" programs are aimed at the financing of so-called "general services," which cover scientific research, pest and disease control, training and re-training services, obtaining professional higher and technical education and general inspection services (including inspecting agricultural raw materials and foodstuffs). Direct payments to farmers based on acreage are also counted as "green box measures" although their usefulness is questioned support for the largest and usually wealthiest farms are very costly. Since 2009, Ukraine has adhered to its commitments on the gradual decrease of export duties for sunflower seeds, live cattle, animal hide and nonferrous metal scrap.

---

[24]This section draws upon the study by Iryna Kobouta, prepared for BRAAC in 2009-2011.

The 2008-2009 global financial crisis came only a few months after Ukraine's WTO accession, and therefore became a serious test for Ukraine's ability to uphold its commitments. Parliament rejected the draft law on customs tariffs, which aimed to reduce import duties for 3,000 items. However, the Custom Service continued to apply tariffs established by the Protocol on the Accession of Ukraine to the WTO that was ratified earlier by parliament. In February 2009 parliament approved a law introducing a 13% surcharge to applied rates of import duties for several goods. The WTO agreement contains no provision that allows a country to implement such duties by blaming the global financial crisis and in June 2009 the WTO Committee on Balance of Payment Restrictions declared them as infringing WTO rules. Ukraine did not renew the surcharges and they expired on September 7, 2009. Nevertheless, in 2010 parliament again attempted to circumvent WTO rules and introduce protective duties for producers of automobiles, refrigerators and some foodstuff products aimed at the protection of the interests of a narrow groups of producers but to the detriment of Ukrainian consumers.

After joining the WTO the Tymoshenko government lifted export quotas for grain, wheat (mixture of wheat and rye), barley, corn, and rye. The restrictions on the export of grain and oil-yielding crops were introduced in 2006-2008 under the pretext of protecting foodstuff prices on the domestic market but damaged the interests of exporters and producers. Tons of grain prepared for export were ruined in ports and warehouses.

The following are the negative consequences resulting from export quotas:

- Decrease in foreign currency inflows to the Ukrainian economy;
- Increase in devaluation pressure on the *hryvnia* that led to increases in costs of imported goods;
- Loss of attractiveness for domestic and foreign investors;
- Long-term decrease in the production of goods subject to quotas.

The image of Ukrainian exporters as reliable suppliers of foodstuffs was ruined. Ukrainian producers were pushed out of profitable markets because they are considered unreliable.

The WTO permits export restrictions in cases of "critical deficiency of foods" (paragraph 2 (a) of Article XI of GATT 1994) which would be rather difficult to prove in the case of grain and sunflower products in Ukraine. Certainly, the export of food products that would benefit from world prices may push domestic prices up. The recipe to deal with this is to keep the indexation of income for poor families to compensate for price increases, and food stamps or other similar measures targeted on poor. The state reserves accumulated in good harvest years can be utilized in poor years to moderate possible price hikes on critical food products.

Unfortunately, the Azarov government resorted to old practices again in 2010 and 2011, when restrictions were introduced through the imposition of extremely bureaucratic measures to control the quality of exported grain. Finally, in October 2010 the government issued a decree introducing an export quota of 2.7 million tons of grain from the beginning of 2011. The export quota for wheat is 0.5 million tons, for barley 0.2 million tons, for corn 2 million tons and quotas for exports of rye and buckwheat of 1,000 tons each.

The other impediment to export activities is the long-standing problem of VAT refunds to exporters. Despite a serious effort to reduce VAT refund arrears through the issuing of VAT bonds and transition to on-time refunds, the problem remains in place.

A Cabinet of Ministers decree from December 13, 2010 establishes a mandatory registration of export contracts for some agricultural goods at the Agrarian Exchange or at exchanges provided with the right to register foreign economic contracts. This Decree distorts market competition and imposes technical barriers to the efficient operation of the agricultural market.

Economic and Trade Impact of the Deep and Comprehensive Free Trade Agreement (DCFTA)

In view of the absence of an EU membership perspective, the DCFTA may become a milestone vehicle for modernization of the Ukrainian economy, if it is signed, ratified and implemented. The DCFTA between Ukraine and EU is not a standard free trade agreement, and from the very beginning it was conceived as a new generation agreement. Besides liberalization of trade, the DCFTA is aimed at deep and comprehensive harmonization of economic legislation. Chief EU negotiator Philippe Cuisson compared the legal status of relations with Ukraine after implementation of the DCFTA with that of Norway or Switzerland. The DCFTA will provide access for Ukrainian companies to EU markets and public procurement meaning that Ukrainian companies can compete on an equal footing in construction work, transportation services, and supply of goods and services for central and local governments throughout the European Union.

In the sphere of trade at least 95% is to be fully liberalized with the elimination of quotas and tariffs. The EU is the largest single market in the world, about 130 times larger than the Ukrainian domestic market and 15-20 times larger than the Russian, Belarus and Kazakhstan markets combined. Free trade between Ukraine and the EU will open up opportunities for deep integration, including in highly specialized intra-industrial integration. Evidence from Central-Eastern European countries proves that open access to the EU market gave enormous stimuli to small enterprises as well as to big business. In 1995-2003, that is after Poland signed the Association Treaty but still before becoming an EU member, exports from Poland to the EU increased 2.6 times.

Ukraine will also become more attractive for foreign investors. Of course, the DCFTA will be an insufficient factor attracting foreign investors to Ukraine. There is also a need for reliable protection of property rights, independent judiciary, and other reforms.

The DCFTA will, however, impose costs on Ukrainian businesses. The most costly rules are to be implemented gradually over a period of time, at least over 10 years, and for some areas even longer. Ukrainian companies will also secure measures protecting them against unfair competition. It is worth pointing out that the Ukrainian market is already relatively open for competition.

When Ukraine changes its legislation and administrative procedures and restructures some of its institutions in order for them to mirror the rules and regulations of the 27 EU member states, the EU will treat Ukrainian institutions as their own and will accept their authority and judgement. It means that products approved in Ukraine will be accepted without any further checks in the EU.[25]

Ukraine can maintain its Free Trade Agreement (FTA) agreements with other countries, including with Russia, Belarus and Kazakhstan. The rules of origin protect unlawful flow of EU goods into other markets through Ukraine, as in all other free trade agreements across the world. However, joining the CIS Custom Union with the Russian Federation, Belarus and Kazakhstan would make the DCFTA with the EU technically impossible. Ukraine cannot be a member of two customs unions. Joining the CIS Custom Union with countries that are not members of the WTO (Russia, Belarus, Kazakhstan) would require a renegotiation of Ukraine's accession agreement with the WTO. FTAs and custom unions with countries that are not members of the WTO, deprived such countries of WTO arbitration in the event of trade disputes. Joining an FTA with any country or group of countries, even those not belonging to the WTO, is compatible with the EU's DCFTA, but membership of the CIS Custom Union is not.

The most disputable part of the DCFTA consists in restrictions to trade in some agricultural products. The EU—as in the case of other FTAs—wants to protect its domestic market for a few agricultural products, but the problem is that some of these are very important for Ukraine. Ukraine was the granary of Europe, as 70% of European black soil is to be found in Ukraine. Ukraine has a large underutilized labor force and excellent climate. According to FAO estimates Ukraine could more than double its agricultural production. The consequences of restrictions in agricultural trade between the EU and Ukraine will be the following:

- EU consumers will be deprived of food supplies that are more diversified in price, assortment, and quality;

- Ukraine will not receive a stimulus to develop its agricultural sector to its fullest potential;

- the best European soils will remain underutilized;

---

[25]Mark Hellyer, *The Ukraine-EU FTA: What's it All About?*, (Kyiv: British Embassy, Kyiv, September 2009), p. 8.

- the worst European soils will be still cultivated because they are subsidized by taxpayers;

- migratory pressure from Ukraine to EU will continue.

The DCFTA is to be reviewed after 5 years. Restrictions in agricultural trade should be lifted at that stage to benefit both sides of the agreement. The vested interests of small groups of the EU farmers that are not competitive, despite the provision of heavy subsidies, should not be permitted to prevail over the interests of European consumers, taxpayers, and the EU's strategic interest in integrating Ukraine into the European economy and structures.

The EU's Association Agreement with Ukraine, including the DCFTA, could be the first of its kind under the European Neighborhood Policy and Eastern Partnership. On October 20, 2011 Deputy Prime Minister Andrey Klyuyev and EU Trade Commissioner Karel De Gucht reached an agreement on all elements of a free trade deal. But—as De Gucht said—"we still have to fine tune some technical details. It is now up to the Ukrainian leadership to create the political conditions wherein this deal can materialize. This should allow us to technically conclude the Association Agreement including the deep and comprehensive free trade area by the end of the year; of course provided that the political conditions are created so that this deal can happen in practice."[26] The EU and U.S. had condemned the sentencing of Tymoshenko to seven years imprisonment on October 11, 2011 and Yanukovych's visit to Brussels planned for nine days later was cancelled by the EU.

Oligarchs and Reforms

Privatizing on advantageous terms, obtaining preferences in lucrative tenders, and limiting internal and external competition are the most widespread arenas within which rent-seeking oligarchs operate in Ukraine. Unlike the Russian oligarchs, who are subordinated to political rulers since Vladimir Putin first came to power in 2000, Ukrainian oligarchs are active in politics and have influence on politicians from various groups. Their political preferences are diverse,

---

[26]http://ec.europa.eu/commission_2010-2014/degucht/.

although they tend to seek to be on good terms with the winning camp. Despite their widespread influence, oligarchs did not prevent an increase in gas prices for the industrial sector or the opening of Ukraine to external competition after the country joined the WTO. Legislation introducing additional tariffs to protect a few inefficient producers in breach of WTO commitments were introduced but after a dispute with the WTO were cancelled. Oligarchs have accumulated enormous assets due to non-transparent privatizations, unclear rules, private connections, and high-level corruption in the government and courts. "The systematic plunder of economic resources, perpetrated under the oligarchic system, has imposed great costs upon Ukrainian societyn" observed Rosaria Puglisi.[27]

Can Ukrainian oligarchs become more interested in the protection of property rights, good legislation, and an independent judiciary? They are certainly afraid of the introduction of the Russian model of relations between political leaders and the business community. Some of them, such as two leading oligarchs Rinat Akhmetov and Viktor Pinchuk, promote European values and rapprochement with the EU through the financing of seminars, events, scholarships, including with reformers in the presidential team. Oligarchs are also becoming aware that developing ties with the EU, and eventually joining the EU, will open new business opportunities and, even more important, will make their assets more valuable. They are also interested in social and political stability, as seen in their facilitation of compromise in the spring 2007 political crisis, when President Yushchenko disbanded parliament, leading to early elections in September of that year. Some Ukrainian oligarchs have recently started to improve their reputation and public relations.

Nevertheless, it would be naive to assume that one day oligarchs will stop abusing opportunities for corrupt rents. Established tycoons might contribute to reforms, but their approach to reforms will remain multifaceted. As Slawomir Matuszak from Poland's Center of Eastern Studies states, "A Majority of the oligarchs treats the association agreement with the EU above all as a way of blocking Russian integration projects and consolidating their political position with

---

[27]Rosaria Puglisi, "The Rise of the Ukrainian Oligarchs," *Demokratization*, Vol. 10, No.3 (Autumn 2003), p. 99.

regard to Russia.(..) The reluctance to sign the agreement is caused by the fear that it will lead to a fierce conflict with Russia.(...) The signing of the DCFTA may be even of advantage to Firtash's interests if it boosted exports of chemical goods to Western countries. The conclusion of the DCFTA will hurt smaller oligarchs, e.g. the owner of the AvtoZAZ car company."[28]

Freedom of media, a parliamentarian system of government and independent NGOs combating corruption could contribute to disciplining oligarchs. It would be also advisable to work with them, including them in meetings with delegations of foreign leaders visiting Ukraine, inviting some to prestigious gatherings, and encouraging them to fund philanthropic educational activities. They need to be convinced of the advantages of an alternative way of doing business than the one to which they have become accustomed.

Conclusions and Recommendations

There have been a number of programs of reforms consisting of lists of recommendations during the two decades of Ukrainian independence.[29] However, the implementation of reforms is very slow. The Tymoshenko cabinet lacked a parliamentary majority, was in conflict with President Yushchenko, and was preoccupied with the upcoming 2010 presidential elections, neglecting difficult reforms. However, the Tymoshenko government solicited a reform program from a group of international experts that would be ready following the presidential elections. These proposals were not used, however, as Tymoshenko lost the 2010 election to Yanukovych.

The Azarov government elaborated a "Presidential" program of reforms entitled "Affluent Society, Competitive Economy, Efficient

[28]Slawomir Matuszak, "How Ukrainian Oligarchs View Economic Integration with the EU and Russia," *EASWEEK*, September 14, 2011.

[29]Affluent Society, Competitive Economy, Efficient State. Program of Economic Reforms for 2010-2014, Committee for Economic Reforms under the President of Ukraine, June 2010; Policy Recommendations on Economic and Institutional Reforms 2009 (Kyiv:EU/UNDP Blue Ribbon Analytical and Advisory Centre, April 2009). Anders Aslund and Oleksandr Paskhaver, *Proposals for Ukraine: 2010—Time for Ukraine*, International team of experts, Kyiv 2010.

State" that was adopted in June 2010. But the program was merely a list of tasks and government capacity in developing modern legislation remains low. Highly qualified lawyers work for private companies, banks and Western foundations—not for the government.

Coordination of foreign assistance is poor. EU donor countries base their plans on directives from their national capitals and perceive the EU-Ukraine Association Agenda as a guide, ignoring the presidential program of reforms. Coordination of foreign assistance was not transferred from the remote Division of Foreign Cooperation at the Ministry of Economy to the Presidential Administration's Committee on Reform that became a hub for generating reform ideas. The Committee on Reform lacks staff to develop draft legislation and government employees are not qualified enough to develop modern economic legislation. Under these circumstances, some external support that would enable the hiring of lawyers and experts from the private sector has been provided by Akhmetov's Foundation for Effective Governance.

Successful adoption of WTO-related regulations or first steps in implementation of the IMF's SBA are important examples of how international organizations can play an important role in reforms. Therefore, it is justified to consider implementation of the DCFTA as a potentially very powerful vehicle for modernization of Ukraine and implementation of reforms. However, the organization of technical assistance will be crucial in making the DCFTA an effective tool for the modernization of Ukrainian legislation and economic institutions.

Cooperation with the IMF as a source of affordable support for the balance of payments, as a generator of confidence for investors in Ukraine, and as a sound and professional point of reference for reforms should be continued. Foreign investors trust in the IMF and appreciate a country's cooperation with this institution. Two politically difficult reforms that Ukraine agreed to undertake with the IMF are pension reform, especially raising the retirement age, and bringing household utility tariffs in line with market prices. Any energy tariff reform should be accompanied with compensatory measures for low income households. Developing energy savings projects with the World Bank and EBRD based on returns from energy savings will bring enormous savings in energy consumption. If added to this there is the elimination of obstacles such as price controls and restrictive licensing for extraction of domestic gas and oil there will be a dramatic increase of Ukraine's energy independence.

Simplified taxation should be introduced for small and medium businesses, to include simplified accounting of revenues with no requirement for primary documents or cash registers. The schedule for an incremental increase in unified tax rates and ceiling in order to adjust them to changes in social welfare and inflation should be based on an indexation linked to the CPI or subsistence level. The one-shot increase in the rates should not exceed 25% each quarter. Previously introduced principles of the "one-stop shop" for registering and licensing businesses, "silent is contest," self-certification and the declaratory principle should be made operational. All types of permits other than those directly stipulated by the law should be abolished. Business associations could play an important role here. The reduced number of permits and activities subject to mandatory licensing should be compiled into a single piece of legislation.

Despite a new law on joint stock companies the corporate legislation that Ukraine still uses is in dire need of reform. The Economic Code of Ukraine, which combines element of the Soviet command administrative economy and market institutions, should be abandoned. The norms of the Civil Code of Ukraine dealing with legal entities should be in compliance with requirements in EU Directives on company law.[30] The law of Ukraine on joint-stock companies should be amended in order to comply with requirements of EU Directives on company law, and internationally accepted principles of corporate law and corporate governance best practices. The main change that is required is to transform the legal model of a joint–stock company from one of "profit-extracting" to "investor protection."[31] There needs to be a separate law on limited liability companies, with an efficient system of governance, control bodies and reliable protection of minority participants in order to provide modern legal structures for the most advanced small and medium enterprises, domestic

---

[30] The text of the draft law could be found at http://brc.undp.org.ua/img/publications/ProposalsCivCode%20.doc.

[31] The text of the draft law developed by BRAAC can be found at http://brc.undp.org.ua/img/publications/JSCAmd2010%20.doc.

and foreign investors.[32] An amendment to the law on re-establishing solvency of a debtor or declaring a debtor bankrupt is also necessary, with provisions that prevent abuses by related-party (conflict of interest) transactions, and that enhance the personal responsibility (liability) of company officers and bankruptcy commissioner in order to prevent abuse of power, while permitting quick sale of businesses.

Ending the moratorium on trading agricultural land and ensuring free access of citizens and agricultural producers to land resources are long overdue actions. Prices for agricultural land should be liberalized and work on establishing a land cadastre should be continued. Allowing access of foreigners and foreign-owned companies to ownership of some agricultural land deposits (e.g. up to 10% of land in each oblast) should be discussed. Such reforms would attract more capital, help to import and disseminate modern agricultural technologies, and facilitate greater access to international channels of distribution of agricultural products.

Administrative restrictions on exports should be abandoned. Targeted income support measures for poor families, as an instrument for compensating the rise in foodstuff prices, should be implemented. The Agricultural Fund and State Reserves can be drawn upon to moderate the domestic impact of price fluctuations on the internal market.

It is in the interest of Ukraine to liberalize global trade in foodstuffs. Ukraine might contribute to enhancing this step through lobbying in the Doha round of multilateral trade negotiations. It would be also useful to establish an information service for agricultural markets that would monitor and forecast the situation on the global food markets and collect information on standards in other countries. Speeding up the harmonization of Ukraine's certification and standardization system with international and European systems, to bring sanitary and safety standards up to the levels of the European Union, are important reforms. Establishing free trade area agreements based on WTO rules with other non-EU trade partners is also in Ukrainian interests. The scandalous problem of delays in VAT refunds for exporters should be urgently fixed.

---

[32]BRAAC has prepared the text of the draft law which is available at http://brc.undp.org.ua/img/publications/Draft_LLC.doc.

The strengthening of programs of social support and re-training programs for redundant leased agricultural workers is also important. Transforming the law of Ukraine on state support of agriculture into a single piece of legislation would simplify and rationalize the question of state support to this important sector of Ukraine's economy.

Chapter Five

Ukraine's Energy Security Challenges: Implications for the EU

Frank Umbach

The decision by the European Union to cancel a high-level meeting with Ukrainian President Viktor Yanukovych on October 20, 2011 was a protest against the jailing of his political opponent and former prime minister, opposition leader Yulia Tymoshenko, who was sentenced to seven years imprisonment, and a signal that such actions threaten Ukraine's integration into the EU. It also highlighted the contradictory policies of the present Ukrainian President and government.

After the second round of presidential elections in February 2010 resulted in a narrow victory of the pro-Russian candidate Viktor Yanukovych, leader of the Party of Regions, he quickly improved Ukraine's relationship with Moscow, suppressed the political opposition and reduced political freedoms, including a tougher scrutiny of mass media.[1] But, instead of becoming too dependent on Russia, President Yanukovych has also sought to follow a "multi-vector foreign policy" by playing a balancing act of Ukraine between Russia and the EU and by using the differences and rivalries between them to strengthen Kyiv's position and leverage.[2] He even chose Brussels for his first foreign visit and declared European integration to be a strategic aim of his presidency. By recognizing Ukraine's independent national interests from Russia's, he had promoted an association

---

[1] See Pavel Korduban, 'Ukrainian President Yanukovych Determined Not to Let Tymoshenko Go,' *Eurasia Daily Monitor*, Vol. 8, Issue 191 (October 18, 2011) and Taras Kuzio, 'Can Ukraine Hold Free Elections Next Year,' *Eurasia Daily Monitor*, Vol. 8, Issue 191 (October 18, 2011).

[2] See also James Sherr, *The Mortgaging of Ukraine's Independence. Briefing Paper* (London: Chatham House, August 2010).

agreement instead of joining a Russian-led CIS Custom Union.[3] In August 2010, President Yanukovych stated:

> I believe Ukraine's future belongs in Europe. While our historical connection to Russia will continue to be very important, the key to prosperity for our people and the development of our national and human resources lies in a deeper and more developed integration with Europe and the West.... Our current exploration of shale and offshore reserves will diversify energy supplies and help avert future crises. Our strong economic ties with the EU will only increase after we finalize an Association Agreement later this year—a springboard to future EU membership.[4]

However, he did not recognize that an association agreement and a closer integration policy with the EU should be based not only on economic interests but also on democratic values and principles that would lead to an "Open Ukraine" as part of a European perspective for his country.

For the EU, the imprisonment of Yulia Tymoshenko has caused a complex dilemma in its relations with Ukraine, because its firm stand on human rights and democratic principles may compromise the EU's wider geo-economic and geopolitical interests and could drive Yanukovych closer into Moscow's arms. Furthermore, the real victim might not be so much the Yanukovych entourage and Party of Regions as an isolated Ukrainian society from Europe, a factor the Ukrainian opposition fears.[5]

Given its size, its geographic position, its population of almost 50 million, and its role as the main transit country for Russian oil and gas

---

[3] See Joshua Chaffin, 'EU Postpones Ukraine Meeting,' *Financial Times*, October 18, 2011 and Stephen Castle and Ellen Barry, 'Europe Cautiously Signals Its Displeasure Over a Prosecution in Ukraine,' *New York Times*, October 18, 2011.

[4] President Viktor Yanukovych, 'Ukraine's Future Is with the European Union. Our Unpredictable Relationship with Russia Has Long Blighted Our Energy Security,' *Wall Street Journal*, August 25, 2011.

[5] See Silke Mülherr, "Janukowitsch isoliert unser Land". Die ukrainische Oppositionspolitikerin Korolewska warnt trotz des skandalösen Timoschenko-Urteils vor einer neuen Eiszeit," *Die Welt*, October 19, 2011.

exports to Europe, Ukraine has always been a critical strategic factor for European and Eurasian security. When the Soviet Union collapsed, Ukraine inherited an economic planning and decision-making system that was previously controlled by Moscow. From the very beginning, Ukraine's energy sector has been plagued not just by an aging infrastructure, inefficiency and widespread corruption, but also by "a disconnect between stated policy priorities and real actions, political games with utility rates during election campaigns, a flawed rate policy, the lack of foreign investment, and energy sector statistics that do not reflect the real situation."[6] These are typical phenomenon of Ukraine's culture as a "momentocracy" where short-term policies and lack of long-term visions dominate the country's elites.

It was only in 2006 that a Ukrainian government approved an "Energy Strategy of Ukraine to 2030" that outlined a vision for its future energy policies. However, government policies often contradicted the strategy's objectives, lacked effective mechanisms for its implementation and any market-oriented competition strategy that would remove monopolies and enact transparent regulations in the energy sector. The 2006 energy strategy envisaged a reduction of per-unit GDP consumption, strengthening government oversight to protect the interests of energy consumers, institutionalizing organizational and legislative changes and reducing Ukraine's energy dependence by increasing the production of domestic oil and gas reserves, modernising energy infrastructures (coal-fired and nuclear plants) and reducing energy consumption (i.e. gas). But the strategy lacked a qualitative approach and failed even to bring quantitative results. Some of Ukraine's figures have even declined in comparison with 2006.[7] Instead of defining its long-term national interests and guaranteeing the country's energy security, Ukraine's energy policies and energy sector became increasingly hostage to internal power conflicts. As Ukrainian energy experts have criticized, "Without investment in Ukraine's energy system, which can only be gained by ensuring a free energy market, the Strategy remains little more than paper wishes."[8]

---

[6] I. Patronyk and I. Zhovkva, *Energy Security Challenges in Ukraine: A Snapshot-2010. Policy Paper* (Kyiv: International Centre for Policy Studies (ICPS), 2010), p. 7.

[7] See also Oleksiy Petrov, *Diagnostic Report: Ukraine's Energy Security and Policy Implementation: Oil and Gas* (Kyiv: ESBS-Project, October 2010).

[8] Patronyk and Zhovkva, op, cit., p. 18.

Even in 2010, Ukraine's energy consumption per unit of GDP was still 3.9 times that of the EU and 2.6 times more than the average GDP energy consumption in the world. Together with Russia, Ukraine is one of the most energy inefficient economies in the world.

The Russian-Ukrainian gas conflicts in 2006 and 2009 have highlighted their direct implications for the EU's energy security and the EU-Russia-Ukraine triangular relationship. During the 2009 gas conflict Russia's disruption of gas supplies not only affected Ukraine, but 17 other European customers. If a gas pipeline supply disruption is taking place, there is hardly any diversification option available in the short-term, whereas a tanker can be re-routed to another oil producing country and/or oil terminal. Hence, pipeline dependencies may have very different crisis management implications for the security of energy supplies.[9]

The first gas crisis in January 2006 led to the birth of the EU's common energy policy. Just one year later, the EU adopted the world's most ambitious and first "integrated energy and climate policy" that focused on the security of the EU's future energy supplies by increasing energy efficiency and conservation and by diversifying energy mix and imports; in particular, due to its forecasted rising demand for gas. Moreover, the EU's new June 2007 Central Asia policy and its Neighborhood Policy in Eastern Europe and Eurasia has been perceived in Russia as a challenge to its own geopolitical interests in the former Soviet Union and South Eastern Europe.[10]

While the EU was hoping that the Orange Revolution would promote and quicken the transition of Ukraine's political and economic system to a democracy and market economy, Moscow perceived the Orange Revolution as a threat to its economic, energy and foreign and security interests in Eurasia and the wider European theatre. When the pro-Russian candidate Yanukovych won the presidential elections in the spring of 2010, Moscow expected a much closer economic and foreign policy orientation by the new Russian-friendly

---

[9] See Frank Umbach, "Global Energy Security and the Implications for the EU," *Energy Policy*, Vol. 38, Issue 3 (March 2010), pp. 1229-1240.

[10] See also Frank Umbach, "Energy Security in Eurasia: Clashing Interests," in Adrian Dellecker and Thomas Gomart eds., *Russian Energy Security and Foreign Policy* (Abingdon and New York: Routledge, 2011), pp. 23-38.

Ukrainian government. While the "Kharkiv Accords" of April 21, 2010 extended the lease of the Sevastopol harbour in Crimea for the Russian Black Sea Fleet until 2042 in exchange for a 30% discount of Russian gas prices and seemed to underline the new political rapprochement in their bilateral relations,[11] it was also the starting point of mutual disappointments.

This chapter will analyze Ukraine's energy policies in the wider context of an "Open Ukraine" vision within the common and competing interests of Ukraine and Russia. I will describe Ukraine's present energy dilemmas and mid- and long-term challenges. In this regard, I will also review the "Kharkiv Accords" as an example of "virtual gas discounts" and explain the on-going crisis in Russian-Ukrainian gas relations. Thereupon I will analyze Ukraine's diversification options for its gas imports and future energy dependence on Russia. Against this background and on-going discussions of Ukraine's choosing between an EU Association Agreement and a Russian-led CIS Customs Union, I will also highlight their strategic implications for Ukraine as the EU's main transit country for Russian gas to Europe. Finally, I will analyze what this means for Ukraine's future reform policies and energy dependency on Russia.

Ukraine's Energy Dilemmas and Challenges

Although Ukraine has oil, gas and coal reserves, it is only able to cover 47-49% of its energy demands. Russia has continued to be the biggest supplier of energy to Ukraine covering 85-90% of oil and 75-80% of natural gas imports.[12] Around half of Ukraine's total energy consumption comes from natural gas. Although Ukraine has larger conventional and unconventional gas resources, without deeper and comprehensive reforms and foreign investments it will unable to increase its domestic production of gas. Similar problems can be found in the coal sector. While Ukraine has coal reserves for another

---

[11]See also Frank Umbach, "The Black Sea Region and the Great Energy Game in Eurasia," in Adam Balcer ed., *The Eastern Partnership in the Black Sea Region: Towards a New Synergy* (Warsaw: demosEUROPA (supported by the Polish Foreign Ministry), 2011), pp. 55-88.

[12]See also Patronyk and Zhovkva, op. cit., p. 21.

100 years, the productivity of coal extraction is very low and its production costs are high.

Without restructuring, modernization efforts and liberalized market reforms, Ukraine will be unable to cope with its energy supply challenges, including reducing its extremely high energy consumption.[13] For Ukraine's energy security, raising energy efficiency is one of the most important tasks and challenges and Kyiv needs to recognize that the cleanest, most reliable and cheapest energy is the energy it doesn't use. Energy efficiency is about delivering sustainable economic growth that minimises economic, environmental and social costs, and thereby, reduces import demands and dependency on foreign suppliers. In 2010-2011, Ukraine's investment in energy efficiency projects increased but still only amounts to US$51 million.[14]

A major pre-condition for enhancing energy efficiency and reforming the energy sector within a market economy is the political will to raise prices. Subsidised gas prices have delayed long-overdue reforms of the country's inefficient and wasteful energy infrastructure, they have fuelled high-price gas imports from Russia, compromising its national energy security and its overall economic competitiveness. Most Ukrainian energy producers have been unable to finance even their replacement investments because their revenues from domestic sales do not cover all of their costs. Most energy prices only cover operating costs but do not include the longer-term costs of security of energy supplies and higher energy imports. Ukraine has never developed specific energy taxes except the value added tax (VAT) of 20%.

The lack of strong market reforms is linked to widespread corruption and politically connected business groups who have taken control of controlling stakes in state-owned enterprises through non-transparent insider privatization deals and other opaque economic activities. These groups and their vested short-term interests are not interested in market reforms and transparent privatization. As a critical Ukrainian study concluded:

---

[13]See also Teyana Kistnyuk, "Energy Efficient Ukraine: Is There a Light at the End of the Tunnel?" *Ukrainian Energy*, August 31, 2011.

[14]See "Investment in Energy Saving Projects Reaches USD 51 mln in 2010-2011," *Ukrainian Energy*, September 12, 2011.

The key players in energy security in Ukraine, those who form or influence the formation of energy policy, include the government, international partners, business, and consumers. None of these players defends the country's national interests, nor have any of them guaranteed its energy security.[15]

As a result, Ukraine will also face an increasing environmental challenge as the share of coal in energy consumption is planned to grow from 22% in its energy mix in 2005 to 33% in 2030, which may double Greenhouse Gas Emissions (GHGE), according to its 2006 Energy Strategy.[16] In this regard, independent energy experts and NGOs in Ukraine have expressed their concerns about the closed and non-transparent update of Ukraine's Energy Strategy until 2030 appealing for a public discussion of proposals and inclusion of independent experts.[17]

The mechanism for adopting appropriate legislation and signing international agreements in the energy sector is ineffective and another factor that has contributed to an inadequate investment climate and the absence of structural reforms in the energy sector. One reason for the failure to attract investments is Ukraine's power grid system. This is essential for both raising energy efficiency and conservation as well as modernizing Ukraine's energy sector, industry and households as well as diversifying its national energy mix by expanding renewable energy sources.

The only sector that has received substantial investments is the nuclear power industry which currently is operating 15 nuclear power blocks in the country. Ukraine is the seventh largest nuclear power producer in the world and the fourth largest in Europe. But, its electricity grid is also aging rapidly and at present, electricity is being exported to only Poland, Hungary, Romania and Slovakia. To increase its electricity exports from 11.35 billion (bn) kWh in 2010 to 25 bn

---

[15]Patronyk and Zhovkva, op.cit., p. 7.

[16]See Patronyk and I.Zhovkva, op. cit., p. 24.

[17]See "Appeal to the President of Ukraine Concerning the Update of the Energy Strategy of Ukraine," *Ukrainian Energy*, October 17, 2011. Available from http://ua-energy.org/en/post/12522.

kWh by 2030 and integrate its power grids with European UCTE standards will only be realistic through massive modernization and investments. In 2010 Ukraine signed agreements with Russia to build two nuclear reactors giving Russia a monopoly on the supply of fuel to Ukrainian reactors until they cease operation and plants producing nuclear fuel will be constructed on the basis of Russian technology. Taking this path, the Ukrainian government gave up the option of receiving alternative deliveries of American or other foreign fuels and technologies[18] and ignored its own energy strategy that calls for the diversification of deliveries of nuclear fuel, as well as technologies. This may result in Russia's complete domination of Ukraine's nuclear energy sector as the energy agreements will not only make Ukraine more dependent on Russia but also threaten its declared and urgent reform policies in the energy sector.

The 2010 "Kharkiv Accords:" Virtual Gas Discounts

On April 21, 2010, Russia and Ukraine signed the "Kharkiv Accords," which extended the lease of the Sevastopol harbor in Crimea for the Russian Black Sea Fleet from 2017 until 2042 in exchange for a 30% discount of Russian gas prices. Despite Yanukovych's claim that the Accords were a success, the new gas deal maintained higher gas prices than those paid by Belgium and Germany. Indeed in summer 2010, Russia had been forced to decrease and de-link at least 15% of its contracted gas supplies to the EU from the oil price as the result of oversupply on the global gas markets. Furthermore, the discount price for Ukraine was not fixed in contracts but granted in discretion of the Russian side. While Russian and Ukrainian leaders claimed the April 2010 gas agreement would give Ukraine's economy a US$40 billion injection until 2019, the actual gas discount and benefits were in reality only "virtual discounts" and "virtual benefits" based on wrong promises. They misled the West in general and the EU in particular, which had been concerned about the security of its own energy supplies.

---

[18]For background of potential nuclear fuel diversification options see also "Diversification of Nuclear Fuel Supply to Ukrainian NPPs" in Diversification Projects in Ukraine's Energy Sector: Progress, Problems, and Ways of Implementation, *National Security and Defence*, no. 6 (Kyiv, Razumkov Centre, 2009), pp. 38-50.

Following the Accords, Russian Prime Minister Vladimir Putin proposed the merger of state gas companies Gazprom and Naftogaz, which are inefficient and non-transparent monopolists. Putin's proposal was received in Kyiv not as a merger but as a takeover that shocked Yanukovych and the Nikolai Azarov government. While the Ukrainian President and government resisted the proposals for a merger in July 2010, they permitted the potential sale of assets from Naftohaz Ukrainy to foreign investors.[19] As U.S. expert Edward C. Chow had earlier predicted:

> What is almost certain is that it will be discovered in a year or two that Ukraine once again owes Russia billions of dollars in past gas debts. This perfectly fits the debt-for-equity dirty privatization model of Russia in the 1990s and of Ukraine even today. Ukrainian debt can then be converted into Russian assets.[20]

Yulia Tymoshenko's seven-year prison sentence, issued on October 11, 2011, was based on charges that she harmed Ukraine's national interests by agreeing to pay Russia an excessively high price for gas in the January 2009 contract. Nevertheless, her political trial was largely politically motivated and the charges against her overlooks the fact that Ukraine's negotiation position at the time was very weak because of its failure to liberalize its energy sector and decrease its gas import dependence on Russia. The "Kharkiv Accords" also reflected the increasing asymmetric nature of the bilateral power balance between Moscow and Kyiv.[21]

The January 2009 gas contract eliminated the opaque gas intermediary RosUkrEnergo (jointly owned by Gazprom and two Ukrainian oligarchs) which allegedly channeled funds to Russian elites as well as to Yanukovych's allies and associates of former President Yushchenko. The elimination of RosukrEnergo removed a large source of corruption.[22] Furthermore, Tymoshenko managed to change the gas contract

---

[19]See also Vladimir Socor, "Ukrainian Government Prepares Public Opinion for Possible Sales of Naftohaz Assets," *Eurasia Daily Monitor*, Vol. 8, Issue 132 (July 11, 2011).

[20]Edward C. Chow, "Neighborly Corporate Raid," *Kyiv Post*, May 7, 2010.

[21]See also Jonas Grätz and Kirsten Westphal, "Die Ukraine in der Energiegemeinschaft: Die Zukunft des Gastransits," *SWP-Aktuell 13* (Berlin), March 2011.

in January 2009 by decreasing the mandated purchase of gas from 53 bcm to 33 bcm per year.

Nevertheless, the Russian "guarantee" to sell on average 40 bcm of gas per year to Ukraine until 2019 is higher than Ukraine's imports in 2009 and 2010.[23] Kyiv is forced to import more (36.5 bcm in 2010 and 40 bcm in 2011) than its present domestic demand is which is around 33 bcm while not being allowed to re-export any of the imported gas. Furthermore, Kyiv learned from the June 2010 energy conflicts that even pro-Russia Belarus, once the Kremlin's staunchest ally, could face energy supply cuts. Besides the price conflict and Gazprom's understandable refusal to accept payment for debt in foodstuffs and other means of payment, the conflict was also an outcome of Russia's political pressure on Belarus to join the CIS Custom's Union and its unwillingness to sign until Moscow lifted custom duties on oil exported to Belarus.

It is understandable that the Yanukovych government wants to increase domestic gas production (which only meets 30% of its domestic demand) and diversify its gas imports (see below). It also explains why EU-Ukrainian energy cooperation in the fields of nuclear safety, integration of electricity and gas markets, security of energy supplies and transit of hydrocarbons and the coal sector has continued.[24]

In the EU, the April 2010 Russian-Ukrainian agreement to guarantee gas transit of 112 bcm of gas annually through Ukrainian territory over the next five years was perceived as an important step forward in reducing the likelihood of gas disputes between Moscow and Kyiv. The capacity of Ukraine's Gas Transport System (GTS) with its 39,800 km of pipelines, 112 compressor pants, 13 underground storage sites (with a total volume of 32 bcm) and 75 compressor stations is currently around 142 bcm per year, albeit its potential capacity could

---

[22]See also Derek Fraser, "What Was Really in Tymoshenko's 2009 Gas Agreement with Russia," *Kyiv Post*, October 12, 2011.

[23]See also E. C. Chow, "Even Azarov Now Admits Ukraine Got a Lousy Gas Deal," *Kyiv Post*, September 3, 2010.

[24]See European Commission, EU-Ukraine Energy Cooperation. Fifth Joint EU-Ukraine Report: Implementation of the EU-Ukraine Memorandum of Understanding on Energy Cooperation during 2010, Brussels, November 22, 2010.

be 175 bcm. If Ukraine's GTS, its "crown jewel," would be modernized with the EU's support, Ukraine could transport more than 230 bcm of gas every year to Europe. In July 2010, Ukraine launched the modernization and upgrading of the first section of the Urengoy-Pomary-Uzhgorod pipeline which carries gas from Western Siberia to the EU. The upgrading should be completed within three years and the costs of $539 million are financed by Naftohaz ($231 million) and the remainder by the European Bank for Reconstruction and Development (EBRD). According to Kyiv's estimates, the total cost to upgrade the Ukrainian gas pipelines transporting Russian gas to Europe will be around $6.5 billion (one-fourth of the South Stream pipeline costs) and seven years are required for this.[25]

The EU needs to also follow very closely any Russian efforts to buy and control Ukraine's gas pipeline network infrastructure. Although the Yanukovych government have blocked Russian efforts to take over Ukraine's gas pipeline network Ukraine's July 2010 adopted law on the gas sector does not prevent foreign monopolies, such as Russia's Gazprom, from operating in the Ukrainian market. The Azarov-government's proposal to separate the GTS and its underground storage sites from Naftohaz Ukrainy and transfer it's partial or full management or ownership to Gazprom could even be ideal for Russia, "who would then gain control over key assets without taking on any of Naftohaz's debts."[26]

The EU needs to take into account that Russia benefits from the uncompetitive and corrupt market in Ukraine. In this regard it is irritating not just for Ukraine, but for the EU's own future energy security, if EU officials such as Marlene Holzer, EU spokeswoman for Energy Commissioner Guenter Oettinger, declare that a takeover of Ukraine's transit gas system would be a purely bilateral matter between Russia and Ukraine.[27] That position not only contradicted EU policy towards Ukraine but also lacked a deeper understanding and any strategic thinking of EU energy security. If Russian efforts are

---

[25]See P. Korduban, "Ukraine Starts Upgrading Gas Pipelines, Hoping for EU Assistance," *Eurasia Daily Monitor*, Vol. 8, Issue 144 (July 27, 2011).

[26]Patronyk and Zhovkva, op. cit., p. 32.

[27]See P. Korduban, "Ukraine Wary of Putin's Proposal to Merge National Gas Companies," *Eurasia Daily Monitor*, Vol. 7, Issue, May 12, 2010.

successful, the EU's dependence on Russia will not only increase further but also deprive the EU of soft power tools in its neighborhood policy and thus have wider foreign policy implications beyond Ukraine.[28]

Yanukovych's New Gas Crisis with Russia

The renewed price conflicts of imports of gas from Russia is a reminder for the EU not just of the previous gas conflicts in 2006 and 2009 but that any energy conflicts between Russia and Ukraine may have severe consequences for the EU as Ukraine is the main transit country for Russian gas supplies to Europe. With 95.4 billion cubic meters (bcm) through Ukrainian pipelines in 2010, these transported 75-80% of EU gas imports from Russia. The latest price conflict raises even more fundamental questions for the EU's future gas policies and gas contracts of European gas companies with Russia.[29]

The reason behind the Ukrainian government's statement to launch a legal challenge over what it should pay for natural gas imports from Gazprom and receive a "fair price" (like other European gas partners of Russia) is linked to Gazprom's and the Kremlin's insistence on "unconditional adherence" of long-term contracts and their linkage to the price of oil and oil products.[30] Even before 2008 and the global financial-economic crisis, many energy and economic experts had questioned whether those long-term contracts and their linkage to oil prices are still justified.[31] While this price linkage could be historically explained, the previous advantage of a cheaper gas pipeline for Europe was in decline relative to Liquefied Natural Gas (LNG) due to technology innovations, a rapidly growing LNG market, more expensive new gas fields in Russia's north (Yamal Peninsula) or even

---

[28]See also Natalia Shapovalova, "The Battle for Ukraine's Energy Allegiance," *Policy Brief, FRIEDE*, No. 55, September 2010.

[29]See also Frank Umbach, "Energy: What Russia's Long-term Gas Contracts Mean for the EU and Ukraine," *Special Report, Geopolitical Information Service* (GIS - www.geopolitical-info.com), October 6, 2011.

[30]See also Roman Olearchyk and Neil Buckley, "Ukraine Poised to Mount Gazprom Challenge," *Financial Times*, August 31, 2011.

[31]See, for instance, Josef Auer, "Gas and Oil Prices End Long-Standing Relationship," *Talking Point-Deutsche Bank Research*, Frankfurt/Main, February 23, 2011.

Barents Sea (Shtokman-project) and more costly undersea pipelines (like North Stream, Blue Stream or the planned South Stream gas pipelines). Russia has no interest to drop long-term contracts in its business strategy, Ukraine has demanded a return to annual gas contracts instead of the 10-year contract concluded in January 2009. In September 2011, the Russian Foreign Ministry argued strongly against Polish Foreign Minister Radoslaw Sikorski's idea for an independent external audit of Russian-Ukrainian gas contracts.[32]

Moreover, those states which are heavily dependent on gas imports from Russia (like the former Warsaw Pact members and successor states of the USSR) are also more interested in diversification of their gas imports and thereby a reduction of imported Russian gas. Therefore, the share of LNG for the EU is expected to increase from 10% in 2009 to more than 24% by 2020.

While the Ukrainian government wants to change the "enslaving gas contract" and reduce its Russian gas imports from 40 bcm in 2011 to 27 bcm in 2012 and even 12 bcm in 2014, Russia has insisted it pay for at least 33 bcm even if Kyiv would reduce its gas imports to zero cubic meters from Russia. Instead of Russia's gas exports to Ukraine, Kyiv wants instead to buy 25-30 bcm of gas from Central Asia at $220 per 1,000 cubic meters compared with $350 from Gazprom in the third quarter and more than $400 in the fourth quarter of 2011. Both Russia's President Medvedev and Prime Minister Putin have repeatedly made clear, any review of Russia's gas contract with Ukraine could only be solved either firstly, by the merger of Naftohaz Ukrainy and Gazprom accompanied by the transfer of ownership of the Ukrainian GTS to Russia's gas monopoly Gazprom or secondly, by Ukraine joining the Russian led CIS Customs Union with Belarus and Kazakhstan.[33] President Yanukovych turned down these two offers, as had other Ukrainian governments,[34] and dismissed the pressure as "humiliating": "We will not allow to talk to us in such a way ... (They)

---

[32]"Russia Deems Unlawful EU's Presumable Audit of 2009 Gas Contracts," *Ukrainian News Agency*, September 8, 2011.

[33]See R. Olearchyk and N. Buckley, "Ukraine Poised to Mount Gazprom Challenge," *Financial Times*, August 31, 2011.

[34]See "Yanukovych Says Ukraine Not Considering Merger between Naftogaz and Gazprom," *Ukrinform*, September 5, 2011 and Robert Coalson, "Putin Visit to Test Ukraine's Resolve on EU Trade Talks," *Radio Free Europe/RadioLiberty*, April 12, 2011.

pushed us in the corner, at first, and then started to dictate terms. Today it humiliates not only me, but it humiliates the state, and I cannot allow it".[35] This harsh statement reflects the difficult dilemma Yanukovych faces, namely that if Russia does not reduce its gas price to Ukraine, the Ukrainian government will have to raise its domestic gas prices, which Yanukovych and the Azarov government seek to avoid in the run up to the October 2012 parliamentary elections, when the popularity of the Party of Regions is declining.[36]

Russia has always demanded that price conflicts be solved by Belarus and Ukraine selling their gas and oil pipelines and other strategic energy infrastructures to Russia. While Belarus was ultimately forced to take this step, the Ukrainian parliament adopted a national law in February 2007 that prevents the selling, leasing or renting of energy infrastructures to foreign countries and companies. The law was adopted by 430 out of 450 deputies, including the Party of Regions. In voting for the law the Ukrainian Parliament recognized that if Russia controlled the Ukrainian gas and oil pipeline network, its entire economy and foreign policy would be controlled by Moscow. However, the 2007 law was undermined in July 2010 by new legislations permitting a restructuring of Naftohaz Ukrainy by separating the GTS and underground gas storage sites for sale to foreign investors, including Gazprom.

In Russia's view, a merger between Gazprom and Naftohaz Ukrainy could only mean absorption and takeover, with Moscow controlling at least 51% of its common shares, rather than a joint venture with equal shares for both sides. Energy and Coal Industry Minister Yuriy Boyko invited the EU to jointly modernize the Ukrainian GTS, but Gazprom's involvement through granting Moscow a majority control of shares of a bi- or tripartite consortium depends on the future state of EU-Ukrainian relations. Following EU and U.S. condemnation of Tymoshenko's imprisonment, it remains unclear if the EU will sign the Association Agreement (which includes the Deep and Comprehensive Free Trade Agreement) with the EU and live up to its obligations as a full member

---

[35] Quoted from P.Korduban, "Ukraine to Seek Better Gas Deal Without Gazprom Merger," *Ukrainska Pravda*, September 5, 2011.

[36] See P. Korduban, "Ukraine-Russia Talks Deadlocked," *Eurasia Daily Monitor*, Vol. 8, Issue 165 (September 9, 2011).

of the European Energy Community (EEC)[37] Kyiv's membership of the EEC since February 1, 2011 extends the EU's internal energy market to Ukraine, including the anti-corruption norms of European law and the separation of energy production from distribution. Based on this, Gazprom cannot manage the Ukrainian GTS. The EU has also included Ukraine in a new "gas ring" of the European pipeline network uniting the fragmented energy markets of southeastern Europe belonging to the EU's "Southern Corridor" project.

It remains to be seen whether Ukraine is ready to join the third energy package of the EU in 2012, as Vasyl Filipchuk, the director of the EU Department in the Ukrainian Foreign Ministry, has claimed, as this appears ever more uncertain followng the EU's protest against Tymoshenko's imprisonment.[38] EEC members are obliged to implement the EU's third energy liberalization package in their gas and electricity markets by January 2015, the implications of which are far-reaching, often underestimated and never fully understood by members of the EEC. They not only have to revise their legislation and adopt secondary legislation but also promote fundamental changes in market structures by introducing market rules.

The 2006 and 2009 Russian-Ukrainian gas conflicts, which were the most severe energy crises since the oil crisis of 1973, were never just price conflicts, as claimed by some Western economic experts and observers. In these two conflicts, as in the Russian-Belarusian cases, Russia always used unresolved price conflicts for its geopolitical ambitions.[39] Ukrainian energy experts believe: "The 'gas factor' is used by Russia for the solution of other problems of bilateral relations and has become a 'classic means' of political pressure on Ukraine."[40]

Since the dissolution of the Soviet Union, Moscow has often used different gas prices, dependent on whether it perceives a particular

---

[37]See also the website of the Energy Community, http://www.energy-community.org/portal/page/portal/ENC_HOME.

[38]See "Gazprom Cannot be Attracted to Management of Ukrainian GTS—Expert," *Ukrainian Energy*, September 20, 2011.

[39]See also John Lough, "Russia's Energy Diplomacy," *Briefing Paper*, Chatham House, London, May 2011.

[40]"Diversification of Sources of Natural Gas Supply in Eurasia" in *Diversification Projects in Ukraine's Energy Sector: Progress, Problems, and Ways of Implementation*, pp. 10-25.

country as friend or opponent of Russia's interest, to keep adjacent former republics within its sphere of influence. Moscow has therefore punished Ukraine, Georgia and the three Baltic states for their pro-NATO and Western-oriented foreign, security and energy policies. This has in turn led to concerns not just in the countries directly affected but also within the remainder of the EU with its evolving common security and foreign policies.

Following the 2004 Orange Revolution, Ukraine was punished with higher gas prices, whereas Yanukovych benefited from 30% price discounts (around $100 for 1,000 cm) through the "Kharkiv Accords." However, in 2010 these discounted gas prices were higher than what German companies had to pay for LNG at "spot prices" and even for Russian pipeline gas, if one excludes the longer transportation costs. Similarly, the Baltic states are paying higher prices for Russian gas than other European countries and companies in Germany, if one excludes the much longer transportation costs to Germany. In 2011, Russia's gas prices for Ukraine increased to $295 for 1,000 bcm in the second quarter and $355 in the third quarter. If Ukraine followed the price formula established for Germany, its price would be reduced by much shorter transportation costs and the $100 discount per 1,000 cubic meters in the "Kharkiv Accords." Based on this calculation, Ukraine would be paying less than Germany but in fact Ukraine is paying $5-6 billion per year arising from the terms of 2009 gas contract with Russia and $60 billion during the next decade.[41]

The "Kharkiv Accords" weakened Ukraine's negotiating position even further. Given the dependence of Ukraine's heavy industries on cheap gas prices, Russia still sees an opportunity to achieve its ultimate goal in its foreign policy, acquisition and control of the Ukrainian pipeline network and other strategic energy infrastructures. The launch of the North Stream pipeline in the midst of the new Russian-Ukrainian price conflict deprives Ukraine of lucrative transit fees in the future by bypassing and isolating Ukraine, Poland and the Baltic states, strengthening the position of Russia in gas price negotiations with Ukraine. Prime Minister Putin declared that 25% of Russia's gas exports to Europe is more stable and hailed "freedom from the dictate of transit states,"[42] the asymmetry of the power balance in Russia's

---

[41]See "Ukraine Seeks "German Price" for Gas from Russia—Ukrainian President," *Worldwide News Ukraine*, September 7, 2011.

favour in future gas negotiations is growing. Ukrainian state energy suppliers may suffer a reduction in sales of about 20% from 2012 as Kyiv fees from gas transit decline.[43]

By pressuring Ukraine with the South Stream pipeline, which would take its gas primarily from the existing Ukrainian gas pipelines to Europe, Russia has signaled that it has no interest in the modernization of Ukraine's aging pipeline infrastructure in a tripartite consortium with the EU. Such an idea was rejected by Prime Minister Putin in summer 2010. Prime Minister Mykola Azarov has reassured the EU and Russia of the fulfillment of the 2009 gas agreement until both sides find a new agreement[44] but the overall intention of the Ukrainian government remains to reduce its energy dependency on Russia. From Moscow's point of view, Ukraine has remained the most unpredictable partner in the former Soviet Union. Thus, another Russian-Ukrainian energy conflict growing out of mutual competing interests and Moscow's geopolitical ambitions may already loom in the near future when Russia's attempts to take control of the Ukrainian GTS would fail.

Ukraine's Diversification Options for its Energy Mix and Natural Gas Imports

Independent Ukrainian energy experts have long criticized official energy policies and the ruling elites for ignoring and overlooking fundamental changes in global energy and gas markets. This concerns the potential for energy efficiency gains and positive results for overall energy security from the expansion of renewables and LNG.[45] President Yanukovych and the Azarov government are investigating alternative options to decrease Ukraine's energy and gas dependency on

---

[42]Quoted following "Nord Stream to Make Supply Disruptions a Thing of the Past," *RT*, September 6, 2011 (http://rt.com) and "Nord Stream: Kyiv Loses Gas Noose," ibid.

[43]See "Nord Stream to Sap Revenue at Ukraine Gas Companies—Fitch," *Bloomberg*, September 9, 2011.

[44]See "Ukraine Will Fulfil 'Gas Agreement Until New Deal Struck with Russia'," *Interfax*, September 5, 2011.

[45]See "Diversification Projects," op. cit.

Russia because the president "wants to remain the independent leader of a sovereign nation, not the governor of a Russian province."[46]

Ukraine's energy cooperation with the EU could become more important for Kyiv by expanding its renewable energy resources (RES) in order to reduce dependency on Russian gas and oil by diversifying its energy mix as well as its fossil-fuel imports. Ukraine has excellent wind resources on its Black Sea coast (in particular in the Crimea and the eastern shores of the Black Sea which is sparsely populated and ideal for large wind farm installations) and possess a declared large potential of unconventional (shale) gas deposits. According to Ukrainian energy experts, the country has a potential wind power of 33 million (m) gigawatt (GW) or 6,000 times more than the total electricity generated by the country's present power system.[47] But by the end of 2010, Ukraine had only 87 megawatt (MW) of installed capacity which is only a small fraction compared with Romania's 482 MW, Germany's 27,124 MW or the U.S., which has 40,180 MW. The expansion of RES is not only hampered by insufficient investment funds but also by a lack of stable legislative framework, unnerving the market and foreign investors in capital-intensive industries; in recent years, regulations in Ukraine's energy sector have changed on an annual basis.

In order to reduce Ukraine's gas dependency on Russia, the Ukrainian government plans to introduce more energy saving programs and replace its gas consumption with domestically produced coal. Moreover, Ukraine seeks to develop offshore gas fields in the Black Sea (portions of its shelf hold about 380 cubic feet), import natural gas from Azerbaijan via Georgia as LNG (2-5 bcm) and Turkmenistan and build an LNG terminal by 2014 (with a capacity of 5 bcm) on its Black Sea coast.[48]

---

[46]Olga Shumylo-Tapiola, "Ukraine and Russia: Ever Closer Neighbors?" *Policy Outlook* (Washington DC: Carnegie Endowment for International Peace, June 8, 2011) p. 2.

[47]See I.Patronyk and I.Zhovkva, Energy Challenges in Ukraine, p. 28.

[48]The Ukrainian LNG-Project to import gas from Azerbaijan is similar to the Azerbaijan-Georgia-Romania Interconnector (AGRI) project, transporting gas from Azerbaijan through Georgia and the Black Sea to Romania. See also Vladimir Socor, "Ukraine and Azerbaijan Mao Out LNG Project via Georgia and Black Sea," *Eurasia Daily Monitor*, Vol. 8, Issue 179 (September 29, 2011).

The Ukrainian government plans to expand domestic gas production to 21.7 bcm in 2012 which might further increase by exploiting its potential unconventional gas resources. In November 2010, the Ukrainian Ministry of Environment and Natural Resources and the National Joint Stock Company (NAK) "Nadra of Ukraine" declared Ukraine had the largest, shale gas deposits in Eurasia and Europe. If these reserves can be confirmed and drilled they could drastically change the Ukraine's dependence on Russian gas. A U.S. study of the impact of shale gas in Europe, for instance, has predicted that the Russian share of European gas consumption (outside the former Soviet Union) could decrease from 26% in 2007 to about 13% in 2040.[49]

The Ukrainian government believes the potential volume of shale gas by mid-2012 is between 10-30 trillion cubic meters (or twice as large as those of its natural gas resources) and has invited foreign investors to develop its shale gas deposits.[50] In February 2011, at the Strategic Partnership Commission of the U.S.-Ukraine Energy Security Working Group, both sides signed a 'Memorandum of Understanding' to establish a framework for technical cooperation that would assess the potential of unconventional gas resources in Ukraine. This agreement brings in the U.S. Geological Survey (USGS) which is currently undertaking a global unconventional gas resource assessment.[51] Lacking technologies, drilling and management experience to exploit its unconventional gas resources, Ukraine's parliament has already passed more investor-friendly legislation to open its domestic natural gas market to foreign shale gas and coal-bed producers. Meanwhile, Exxon Mobile, Chevron, Total, Eurogas (a U.S. company), TNK-BP and Royal Dutch Shell have announced they will conduct exploratory tests and feasibility assessments.

If anticipated shale gas resources can be explored at reasonable prices, they would offer the most important diversification options to

---

[49] See Kenneth B. Medlock III, Amy Myers Jaffe, Peter R. Hartley, "Shale Gas and U.S. National Security" (James A. Baker III Institute for Public Policy, Rice University, 2011), p. 45.

[50] "Ukraine Claims to Possess World's Biggest Shale Gas Deposits," *PR Newswire*, November 29, 2010.

[51] "U.S.-Ukraine Unconventional Gas Resource MOU Signed," Embassy of the United States, Kyiv, Ukraine, February 15, 2011.

reduce Ukraine's gas dependency on Russia and Gazprom. If the "silent revolution" of new drilling technologies for unconventional gas resources will take place also outside the U.S. it would have fundamental implications for the world's future gas supplies and business strategies. According to the IEA, unconventional gas could cover more than 40% of the global increase of gas demand up to 2035 and would be the major reason for a "Golden Age" of conventional and unconventional gas.[52]

The advantage of unconventional gas is that it is a domestic, national source of fuel supply enhancing the energy security of each country that is not subsidized like renewables, nuclear power and coal. For both the EU and Ukraine, it could become the most important diversification option for their future gas supplies and would increase the security of their energy supplies.[53] Unconventional gas also gives buyers more leverage to renegotiate the high Russian oil-indexed gas price demands that are included in long-term contracts that are an obstacle for a European and Ukrainian expansion of unconventional gas, given Russia's strategic interests and the leverage it has towards its gas partners.

The Russian government and Gazprom try to downplay the importance of shale gas in Europe and Ukraine and point to very negative implications of unconventional gas production for the environment.[54] If Ukrainian and European gas policies remain hostage to long-term contracts, "take-and-pay"-clauses and the oil price linkage (even when international gas markets have been de-linked from oil price markets), new and sustainable integrated energy and climate policies cannot be implemented as their energy mix and gas volumes will remain fixed

---

[52]See International Energy Agency (IEA), "Are We Entering a Golden Age of Gas," *Special Report. World Energy Outlook 2011*, 2011.

[53]See also Maximilian Kuhn and F. Umbach, "Strategic Perspectives of Unconventional Gas in Europe: A Game Changer with Implications for the EU's Common Energy Security Policies," *EUCERS-Strategy Papers*, King's College, Vol. 1, No. 1 (May 2011).

[54]"Alexander Medvedev Answers Your Questions—Part One," *Financial Times*, February 18, 2011; "Gazprom Chief Steps Up Attacks on Shale Gas', ibid., February 18, 2011, "Gazprom Chief Calls Shale Gas a 'Bubble'," *Financial Times*, February 18, 2011, and Andrey Konoplyanik, "The Economic Implications for Europe of the Shale Gas ReVolution," *Europe's World*, January 13, 2011.

over the next 25 years or longer. For Ukraine, those long-term contracts and "take-and-pay"-clauses have a considerable short-term impact and implications which the EU should not overlook and ignore. These diversification projects may come too late or cannot be implemented because of their high costs (i.e. LNG options). Moscow may have already succeeded in acquiring a majority control of the Ukrainian GTS in a tripartite consortium with a German company (dependent on Gazprom), leaving Ukraine with only just 20% of the shares.[55] If this would turn out to be the case, Ukraine's sovereignty and independence would come under threat and undermine future democratic and market reforms. In addition to this, such a development would have considerable geo-economic and geopolitical implications for the EU's energy security and foreign policy.

Conclusions and Perspectives for an "Open Ukraine" in Energy Policies

As Ukraine's domestic policies and non-democratic tendencies indicate, Kyiv's future relationship with the EU will remain difficult and uncertain. Tymoshenko's imprisonment highlighted "selective justice," subservience of the judicial system to the executive power and the return of political persecution to Ukraine. For a large part of the Ukrainian population and the West, Yanukovych government and the emerging Ukrainian regime have nothing to do with Western standards of democracy, freedom of speech, independent courts, rule of law, transparent political processes and fair elections. Influential Ukrainian oligarchs have no interest in transparency of their business activities and market reforms. Ukraine's intentions to integrate with the EU is not based on shared democratic values but arises out of not becoming too dependent on Russia, albeit Russia will remain the country's main trading partner in the near future.

An "Open Ukraine" as an increasingly integrated associated partner country of the EU needs to implement structural market reforms in order to enhance transparency as a pre-condition of economic competitiveness and energy security. If energy and gas prices remain low they

---

[55]See P. Korduban, "Ukraine and Russia Prepare New Gas Agreement," *Eurasia Daily Monitor*, Vol. 8, Issue 178 (September 28, 2011).

will further hamper any larger and substantial energy reforms aiming to increase energy efficiency and conservation. By utilizing Soviet-era legislation against his political opponents, President Yanukovych has brought his country into a collision course with the EU.

Even with a pro-Russian president of Ukraine, Kyiv's energy, economic orientation and foreign policies have been disappointing for Russia given its great hopes that Ukraine would return within its sphere of influence. Russia is only interested in joining a bi- or tripartite consortium of the Ukrainian GTS if it were to gain a dominant role through control of the majority of shares. Russia is not interested in a consortium with equal shares for participants. Yanukovych believes he already made many concessions with Russia on recognition of the 1933 famine) as a "genocide," NATO membership and the Russian Black Sea Fleet base. But, these steps appear only to have increased Moscow's appetite in Ukraine. Progress in Russian-Ukrainian relations would seem to be impossible without accepting Russia's economic domination through membership in the CIS Customs Union or by Russia taking control of the Ukrainian GTS. From Yanukovych's point of view, despite his concessions and pro-Russian attitudes he has received almost nothing in return and Russia still does not accept and respect Ukrainian sovereignty and independence.[56]

Ukraine's official accession in February 2011 to full membership of the EU-sponsored Energy Community treaty was an important step towards growing energy cooperation with the EU. But given Yanukovych's domestic power base and his close ties to Ukrainian oligarchs and their vested interests in a non-transparent business environment, deep-rooted structural market reforms are unlikely to materialize. Ukraine's commitments under its European Energy Community membership to liberalize its energy markets and implement key EU legal acts seems unlikely therefore in the near future. These include fundamental reforms in its energy sectors towards a "pan-European market, based on the principles of solidarity and transparency."[57]

---

[56]See also T. Kuzio, "Poor Ukrainian-Russian Ties Reflect Yanukovych-Putin Relationship," *Eurasia Daily Monitor*, Vol. 8, Issue 180 (September 30, 2011).

[57]See Umbach, "The Black Sea Region...," op. cit., pp. 75.

Although Yanukovych has followed a "multi-vector foreign policy" by playing a balancing act between Russia and the EU, his multi-vectorism is far more limited than Kuchma's. He can no longer use the NATO card and has given away the jewel in the crown (Sevastopol) for a "virtual" gas discount. But this multi-vector foreign and energy policy has now come to an end as the Ukrainian authorities need to choose between a re-orientation towards Russia and entering the Russian-led CIS Customs Union. If Kyiv chooses the latter option the path will block domestic market reforms and Association Agreement with the EU which offers a path towards closer integration with the EU and stabilizing the country's long-term energy security. Simultaneous membership of the CIS Customs Union and EU Association Agreement is impossible. Only the Association Agreement would ensure future competitiveness, transparency and accountability in Ukraine's energy market, offer greater investment in infrastructure and new technologies and thereby decrease the country's dependency on gas imports from Russia. Two U.S. experts concluded that "Partnership with the EU is not a silver bullet for the troubled Ukrainian energy sector, but it is certain to reduce the volatility of future pricing disputes and is perhaps the only solution that does not leave Ukraine's fate entirely in Russian hands."[58]

While the EU and European Parliament have expressed their concern about the direction of the president's and government's anti-democratic tendencies and deterioration of human rights in Ukraine the country is too important for the EU's future energy security to be isolated. But the stakes are also high for Ukraine as the EU is Ukraine's main commercial partner accounting for a third of its total external trade. While Ukraine no longer seeks NATO membership, Kyiv's aspiration for EU membership remains a declared goal, although rhetoric means very little if it is not backed up by policies. Domestic policies under four Ukrainian presidents have never been consistent with their declared goals in the energy field.

Given its present weak economic and political position vis-a-vis Russia, Ukraine needs to be offered in the future new economic and

---

[58]Richard B. Andres and Michael Kofman, "European Energy Security: Reducing Volatility of Ukraine-Russia Natural Gas Pricing Disputes," *Strategic Forum* (INSS), February 2011, p. 14.

political incentives from the EU and the U.S. to avoid a further deterioration of the European-Ukrainian relationship. Traditionally, energy security has been one of the weakest links in Ukraine's national security strategy. In the words of Prime Minister Azarov:

> The dire state of the Ukrainian economy should provide the EU with the necessary impetus to act. Time is a factor as Ukraine's negotiating position continues to weaken. Ukraine cannot be viewed as a business opportunity alone, rather as a long-term partner imperative to ensure European energy security. Without greater EU investment, Gazprom will likely force Ukrainian cession of ownership rights over its pipeline network in future negotiations over gas prices and modernization.[59]

However, despite the EU's wider geo-economic and geopolitical interests for a close relationship with Ukraine, particularly with regard to energy cooperation, the signing of an Association Agreement cannot be completely decoupled from European values and democratic principles. This is something the Ukrainian authorities still have to learn and to recognize.

---

[59]Quoted following James George Jatras, "Ukraine's Energy Policy: Strategic Path or Tactical Squirming?" *Global Security News*, April 28, 2011.

Chapter Six

Ukraine and European Integration

Péter Balázs[1]

The Economy

Ukraine was hit hard by the global economic and financial crisis. The combination of weaker demand from Ukraine's trading partners, falling export prices, rising import prices and reduced access to international financial markets led to a sharp drop of GDP in 2008 and 2009 (-14.8%). Import and export flows have been compressed and the trade deficit has also fallen sharply. Table 1 also shows that inflation slowed down in 2009 but remained in double digits (15.9%). Unemployment increased to 8.8% in 2009. The *hryvnia* lost almost half of its value against the U.S. dollar since July 2008.[2]

Table 1. Main Economic Indicators for Ukraine

	2007	2008	2009	2010**	2011**	2012**
Real GDP (%)*	7.9	1.9	-14.8	4.2	4.5	4.9
Inflation rate (%)*	12.8	25.2	15.9	9.4	9.2	8.3
Unemployment (% of total labor force)*	6.4	6.4	8.8	8.1	7.8	7.2
Current account balance (% of GDP)*	-3.7	-7.1	-1.5	-1.9	-3.6	-3.8

*Source: IMF (*World Economic Outlook, April 2011*).
**IMF estimations.

---

[1] This chapter was prepared by the Center for EU Enlargement Studies in Budapest and contains contributions from Péter Balázs, András Deák, Áron Szele and Antónia Molnárová.

[2] European Bank for Reconstruction and Development: Ukraine—Key Developments and Challenges: http://www.ebrd.com/pages/country/ukraine/key.shtml.

Table 2. GDP of Selected Countries

Real GDP (%)*

	2007	2008	2009	2010**	2011**	2012**
Ukraine	7.9	1.9	-14.8	4.2	4.5	4.9
Russia	8.5	5.2	-7.8	4	4.8	4.5
Germany	2.8	0.7	-4.7	3.5	2.5	2.1
Hungary	0.8	0.8	-6.7	1.2	2.8	2.8
Poland	6.8	5.1	1.7	3.8	3.8	3.6
Slovakia	10.5	5.8	-4.8	4	3.8	4.2
Czech Republic	6.1	2.5	-4.1	2.3	1.7	2.9

*Source: IMF (*World Economic Outlook Database*).
**IMF estimations.

To restore financial and economic stability in Ukraine, in November 2008 the IMF approved a two-year stand-by arrangement in the amount of a $16.5 billion loan.[3] Another agreement was signed with the IMF in July 2010.

However, the economic situation has improved since 2010. For 2011, the World Bank has raised its forecast for Ukraine's economic growth to 4.5% and GDP is expected to grow by 4.9% in 2012. The European Bank for Reconstruction and Development (EBRD) has also improved its assessment of the economy to grow by 5% in 2011. This reflects improving conditions in the Ukrainian economy and the country emerging from the 2008-2009 crisis.[4]

Table 2 shows economic growth in Ukraine since the outbreak of the global economic and financial crisis in comparative perspective with Russia, Germany and the Visegrad Group of countries. Table 2 shows that in 2009, when the global recession was deepest, GDP growth in all countries, except Poland, was negative but with the biggest decline in Ukraine that was almost twice that experienced by Russia.

---

[3] IMF press release No. 08/271: http://www.imf.org/external/np/sec/pr/2008/pr08271.htm.

[4] Centre for Eastern Studies OSW: A positive economic forecast for Ukraine, July 27, 2011: http://www.osw.waw.pl/en/publikacje/eastweek/2011-07-27/a-positive-economic-forecast-ukraine.

Trade and Foreign Investment

Ukrainian exports to the EU are to a very large extent liberalized due to the Generalized System of Preferences (GSP) granted by the EU to Ukraine since 1993. Following WTO membership in May 2008, the EU and Ukraine launched bilateral negotiations for a Deep and Comprehensive Free Trade Agreement (DCFTA) that would replace the Partnership and Cooperation Agreement signed in 1994 (going into effect following parliamentary ratification by EU members in 1998). The DCFTA is designed to deepen Ukraine's access to the European market, modernize the economy and encourage European investment in Ukraine. Negotiations between the EU and Ukraine were planned to be finalized under the Polish Presidency of the European Council in December 2011 but this could be suspended in retaliation for the trial and sentencing to imprisonment of opposition leader Yulia Tymoshenko on October 11, 2011.[5] The case will make ratification of the Association Agreement by the European Parliament and 27 EU member parliaments difficult.

Ukraine is one of the biggest and, at the same time, poorest countries in Europe, although it possesses vast potential. As Table 3 shows, Ukraine has a relatively low per-capita GDP even among the Eastern Partnership countries. In comparison, Ukraine lags behind the Western Balkan countries (i.e. Albania, 3800 USD) or CEE countries at the time of their respective associate status.

Ukraine has an open economy, with total foreign trade accounting for 81% of GDP and exports/GDP ratio equal to 0.44. The geographic distribution of Ukraine's foreign trade is relatively balanced between East and West, with Russia taking a slightly bigger share both in exports and imports than the EU. Russian imports are mainly energy-related with the gas import bill 45% of total imports. Exports are heavily dominated (up to 60% by metallurgical and related products that are primarily exported to the EU. Energy imports do not impact directly and significantly on the performance of exports as the share of gas among inputs into metallurgy is low.

---

[5] European Commission, DG Trade, http://ec.europa.eu/trade/creating-opportunities/bilateral-relations/countries/ukraine/.

Table 3. Gross Domestic Product Per Capita in EaP and Some Selected Countries

Current prices, 2009 USD

Country	GDP/capita	Ratio in HU level
Armenia	2614.70	0.20
Azerbaijan	4798.24	0.37
Belarus	5190.79	0.40
Georgia	2455.37	0.19
Moldova	1524.23	0.12
Ukraine	**2568.65**	**0.20**
Czech Republic	18170.87	1.41
Germany	40831.66	3.17
Hungary	12893.96	1.00
Russia	8614.03	0.67
Turkey	8711.16	0.68

*Source: International Monetary Fund.

Table 4. Ukraine's Major Foreign Trade Partners, 2010

Billion USD

	Russia	EU	Other
Exports	13.43	13.05	19.62
Imports	22.2	19.1	14.94

Source: Ukranian Statistical Office.

Unlike foreign trade, the EU has a major role in foreign investments into Ukraine with 79% of foreign direct investments from the EU-27 (with 28% of this is from Cyprus). Net inflow was in a range of $5-10 billion during the last five years, a very high level for a CIS non-energy economy. Foreign investment is important because it sets the milestones for further DCFTA implementation and creates strategic corporate actors interested in Ukraine's further European integration. The banking and finance sector is almost completely under foreign ownership. Foreign investors have also moved into the foodstuffs sector, as in Russia and some other CIS states. Ukraine has a good record of integration into the world economy compared to other CIS countries and a big potential for growth due to its size, large population and low level of GDP.

Russia has lobbied for Ukraine's accession to the CIS Customs Union of Russia, Belarus and Kazakhstan. While free trade with Russia has an unambiguous rationale from Kyiv's perspective, the Custom Union—apart from its negative consequences for EU integration— would be beneficial only for some selected industries, such as machine-building. Understandably, the Yanukovych administration does not want to close this door and therefore has kept the discussion on Ukraine and the Custom Union alive in exchange for energy concessions. At the same time, Russia has not been ready to provide Ukraine with a free trade status without Ukraine also entering the CIS Customs Union. Such a step would further complicate negotiations between EU and Ukraine.

Energy

Ukraine's bargaining position in gas transit and imports issues vis-à-vis Russia has been gradually deteriorating. Transit volumes have been decreasing since the first pipe of the North European Gas Pipeline was commissioned (via the Baltic Sea) and since the 2009 gas war that produced a contract whereby Ukraine would be paying European prices (even with a Russian discount). Non-transparency in the Russian-Ukrainian energy relationship makes it difficult to analyze Ukraine's energy sector.

Nevertheless, the following four points should be considered.

First, Ukraine's current gas import bill (even at discounted prices) is an extremely heavy burden for the country as it comprises 7-8% of GDP in comparison, for Hungary it comprises around 3%). Sustainability of these price levels in the current macroeconomic situation is highly questionable.

Second, Russia does not want to give any further price concessions. The Russian state gas company Gazprom publicly stated that price cuts are only possible in exchange for control over property Ukrainian energy assets, such the state as company Naftohaz Ukrainy or the pipeline system (that is, the Belarusian and Armenian models).

Third, EU companies do not want to control energy assets or provide financial assistance to the modernization of the Ukrainian pipeline system. Gazprom is not very supportive and profits will decline in coming years. The energy sector is corrupt and heavily regulated by the Ukrainian authorities. Without a clear positive signal from Russia, an idea of future plans and readiness to welcome Western partners and Ukrainian guarantees on regulation, Western investors will not invest into Ukraine's energy sector. Despite public announcements, there are no prospects for large-scale Western investment into, or assistance for, the Ukrainian pipeline system, except for symbolic aid and loans from the European Commission (that were bundled with certain conditionality requirements).

Fourth, Ukrainian adoption of EU regulation practices will generate conflicts in the Ukraine-Russian energy relationship. Gazprom very much relies on long-term contracts on pipeline capacities while the philosophy of EU regulations is based on third-party access and short–term capacity allocations. Kyiv may prefer to adopt EU-regulations and, at the same time, seek to "overwrite" past contracts with Gazprom. Russia is very much against dividing Naftogaz according to the European unbundling model or providing third-party access, suspecting Ukraine of undermining existing trade and transit patterns unfavorable to its position.

Thus, the key question is the manner in which the Ukrainian authorities will implement the EU *acquis* in the field of energy. A possible solution could be the Central-Eastern European model where long-term Russian contracts enjoyed temporary derogation from EU-regulation following these countries EU accession. Another alternative could be a shallower implementation of European regulatory practices. However, it is reasonable to assume that for Kyiv one of the main benefits of adopting EU regulations is to counterbalance Russia, while patience and tolerance is scarce in Moscow. The threat for the European Commission and EU members is that they involved in any energy conflict where Western actors do not have real influence, while at least one of the parties will refer to existing agreements with the EU.

On the basis of the factors mentioned above, the Ukraine-Russia gas dispute will continue. Yanukovych refused to follow Belarus and Armenia in bowing to Russian demands even if negotiations still cushion the tensions. However, there is a Rubicon that Russia would like to cross; namely obtaining majority control over the Ukrainian

Figure 1. Global View of International Student Origins, 2009/10

Students in the U.S.:
- 72,000 -130,000
- 24,000 - 29,000
- 5,000 - 16,000
- Less than 5,000

Source: http://www.iie.org/Research-and-Publications/Open-Doors/Data/International-Students.

pipeline system. Such an objective might cause further large-scale conflicts between both sides.

Education

Ukraine is not well connected to the European or American educational systems. Such networks are normally at the level of higher education through a number of scholarly networks and funding, such as scholarship opportunities. Improved networks would improve the social and psychological attitudes of Ukraine's younger generation and improve the academic level at Ukrainian academic institutes.

Statistically, Ukrainian students are present in the United States in low numbers—under 5,000 in 2010 (see figure 1).

Similarly, enrollment in EU higher education institutions is very small. A case-study for this is the UK where Ukraine is not among the top ten donor countries, being again in the sub-4000 sender category (see table 5).

Ukrainian higher education institutions are also not members of the Erasmus Mundus network. Establishing a connection to this academic network of exchange scholarships would be important for student mobility and improvement of teaching methodology.

Table 5. Top 10 Non-EU countries That Send Students Abroad

Top 10 non-EU senders	2009-10	2008-09
China (PRC)	56.990	47.035
India	38.500	34.065
Nigeria	16.680	14.380
United States of America	15.060	14.345
Malaysia	14.060	12.695
Hong Kong (Special Administrative Region)	9.945	9.600
Pakistan	9.815	9.610
Saudi Arabia	8.340	5.205
Canada	5.575	5.350
Thailand	5.505	4.675

Source: UK Council for international Student Affairs, http://www.ukcisa.org.uk/about/statistics_he.php#table4).

Table 6. Gross Enrollment Ratios in Tertiary Education by Sex, 1991–2009
Percent

	1991	1999	2002	2009	2009 regional average
Male/Female	47	47	57	81	65**
Male	—	44	52*	72	57**
Female	—	50	62*	91	73**

Source: UNESCO Institute for Statistics, http://stats.uis.unesco.org/unesco/TableViewer/document.aspx?
ReportId=121&IF_Language=eng&BR_Country=8070&BR_Region=40530).

Among existing funding and scholarship opportunities, there is DAAD (German Academic Exchange Service), The Fulbright Program and Visegrad Fund,[6] that has taken an active role in regional collaboration. The Visegrad Fund's activities aim to improve regional collaboration and extend influence under the EU's Eastern Partnership. A component of the Visegrad Fund's educational opportunities offered to Ukraine is the Central European University and multiple educational and research programs.

The number of students remains very small, when compared to the number of students in tertiary education, which was 2,296,221 in the same year. The Ukrainian government spends approximately 5.4% of

---

[6] http://visegradfund.org/scholarships/.

GDP on education, about 20%, which in comparison with other countries is very good, but still small when compared to the actual country's GDP.

We may therefore conclude that Ukrainian higher education lacks sufficient interconnection and networks with international educational facilities.

Ukraine and the Visegrad Group

Ukraine's relations with the Visegrad countries are of unique importance due to geographical and historical reasons. In the 1990s the four countries had close economic ties with Ukraine in the Soviet Union and was their major foreign trade partner (links with Romania also show similarities to the V4–Ukrainian relations). The Visegrad countries remain important trading partners for Ukraine.

The share of the V4 in Ukrainian exports and imports of goods from and to the EU 27 is between 25-30%, with Poland in first place. The figures in Table 7 show that the share of the V4 and Poland's leading role have remained stable. The Hungarian share of Ukrainian exports and imports is rather modest, but interestingly, Ukraine's trade balance in goods with Hungary has recently changed from positive to negative. The share of Slovakia and Czech Republic is marginal and surprisingly, exports from the Czech Republic, a non-neighboring country with Ukraine, surpassed exports from Slovakia in 2010.

Overall, the share of the V4 in total Ukrainian foreign trade turnover is significant. Nevertheless, Ukraine's major trading partners from the EU-27 remain in Western Europe, such as Germany and Italy. However, it must be noted that Ukrainian customs statistics should be treated with caution because they may not always reflect the real state of affairs. Official counterpart statistics from the Visegrad countries are contradictory and there are cases when Ukrainian data is higher or vice versa, probably due to tax-avoidance schemes on the Ukrainian side.[7]

---

[7] Ludvig Zsuzsa, "What may the Visegrad countries offer to Ukraine with special regard to Hungary," in Gábor Fóti and Zsuzsa Ludvig, eds., *Eurointegration Challenges in Hungarian-Ukrainian Economic Relations* (Budapest: Institute for World Economics of the Hungarian Academy of Sciences, 2005), pp. 225-248.

Table 7. Ukraine's Foreign Trade in Goods with the Visegrad Countries

Million USD

	Export 2010	Import 2010	Balance	Export 2009	Import 2009	Balance	Export 2008	Import 2008	Balance
EU 27 total	13051.9	19101.2	-6049	9499.3	15392.7	-5893	18129.5	28868.4	-10739
Italy	2412.4	1390.3	1022.1	1227.6	1139.8	87.8	2911.7	2432.1	479.6
Germany	1499.5	4605.3	-3106	1248.1	3852.1	-2604	1837.1	7165.3	-5328.2
Poland	1787.2	2788.8	-1002	1208	2170.3	-962.3	2338.3	4280.3	-1942
Hungary	860.1	1214.6	-354.5	730.2	678.3	51.9	1367.1	1282.7	84.4
Czech Rep.	626.2	747.9	-121.7	340.7	622.2	-281.5	670.8	1376	-705.2
Slovakia	568.2	442.6	125.6	433.7	306	127.7	910.2	742.5	167.7
V4 total	3841.7	5193.9		2712.6	3776.8		5286.4	7681.5	
in % of EU 27	29.4	27.2		28.6	24.5		29.1	26.6	

Source: Ukrainian Statistical Office (www.ukrstat.gov.ua).

Economic ties are also reflected through foreign capital movements. The share of the Visegrad countries in total FDI invested into Ukraine has been marginal, lower than their share in trade flows. The main foreign investors in Ukraine are Russia, the U.S. and Western European countries (the list also includes some offshore tax havens such as Cyprus and the Virgin Islands, with Russian and Ukrainian capital re-entering Ukraine through them).

From the V4, Poland is the biggest investor in Ukraine, followed by Hungary. However, Hungary no longer appears on the list of countries with the largest investment into the Ukrainian economy, even though data for Hungarian outward investment shows that Central-Eastern European countries (including the Western Balkans) are among its major destinations. The greatest Hungarian investment is into Hungarian small and medium enterprises in the Transcarpathian region, where there are partners within the Hungarian ethnic minority.[8]

---

[8] Ibid.

Table 8. Foreign Direct Investment in Ukraine

Million USD

	FDI as of 1.1.2011	in % of the total	FDI as of 1.1.2010	in % of the total
Total	44708	100	40026.8	100
Cyprus	9914.6	22.2	8593.2	21.5
Germany	7076.9	15.8	6613	16.5
Russia	3402.8	7.6	2674.6	6.7
Virgin Islands	1460.8	3.3	1371	3.4
USA	1192.4	2.7	1387.1	3.5
Italy	982.4	2.2	992.2	2.5
Poland	935.8	2.1	864.9	2.2
Hungary			675.1	1.7

Source: Ukrainian Statistical Office (www.ukrstat.gov.ua).

Towards an Open Ukraine

Energy

Despite controversy, Ukraine is one of the success stories in EU–CIS countries relations. Kyiv joined the WTO, has negotiated a DCFTA with the EU, is open to foreign investment and relatively democratic. Economic growth will be crucial to Ukraine's future Ukraine and low GDP per capita levels will set constraints for further co-operation and limits to integration capabilities.

There are no influential strategic actors in Ukraine fully committed to EU-integration; those that exist are politically weak. Domestic business groups should be interested in opening up exports and receiving access to EU-related funds and partners, although corporate actors and the general political culture of the Ukrainian population is protectionist. For political actors the gap between domestic conditions and ambition remains far too wide.

At the same time, EU-Ukraine relations are crucial for Kyiv even without the prospect for accession for three reasons that provide the EU with real influence over Ukrainian matters. First, the EU is a significant economic and political partner, which could provide real benefits. Second, counterbalance against Russian interests. Third, important source for domestic legitimization.

Russia is neither interested, nor capable of solving Ukraine's economic problems. There is a capacity constraint on both the Western and Russian side. Ukraine needed both IMF-loans and Russian gas price concessions in order to maintain its economic situation. Given the vulnerability of the Ukrainian economy it is reasonable to formulate policies based on three assumptions. The first is that Kyiv needs both Russia and Western support in order to sustain economic and political order. The second is that neither of the parties has enough potential, resources and ambitions to integrate Ukraine. The third is that even if it is not acknowledged, both sides are needed to sustain Ukraine's economic and political growth and stability.

Domestic policies in Ukraine will remain a perennial source of problems for EU-Ukraine relations because Ukrainian politics will continue to be characterized by a mixture of weak statehood, authoritarian reflexes and oligarchic corporate interests. Short-term improvements are unlikely and therefore the EU will need to formulate a medium to long-term strategy in the field of economic growth, energy, and democratic institutions.

Ukraine and the EU

Relations between the EU and Ukraine have intensified since the 2004 Orange Revolution which opened a new chapter in Ukraine's history as an independent state. Orange forces had set out to quickly integrate Ukraine into Euro-Atlantic structures, position the country as a regional leader and promoter of democracy and regional integrator in the post-Soviet space. Despite Ukraine's Western orientation the Orange Revolution failed to bring any changes in the EU policies (see chapters by Stephen Larrabee and Serhiy Kudelia).

Beside the general conditions set out in the EU's founding treaty in articles 6 and 49, which state any European country which respects the principles of liberty, democracy, respect for human rights and fundamental freedoms and the rule of law may apply to become a member of the Union, the EU has never offered any membership perspective to Ukraine. Unfortunately, Ukraine's 2004 democratic breakthrough came when the EU was enlarging into the post-communist world and going through an institutional crisis after rejection of the draft EU constitution by France and the Netherlands.

The EU developed the European Neighborhood Policy (ENP) as a framework policy for relations with the entire EU neighborhood, including Ukraine. The "carrot" of the ENP, defined as a stake in the EU's internal market, brought countries such as Syria, Libya and Belarus into the same policy group as Ukraine which disappointed the pro-European sectors of Ukrainian elites and society.

In 2009, the EU launched the Eastern Partnership, the Eastern dimension of the ENP framework, which provided Ukraine with an opportunity to become a regional leader on European integration as the most advanced of the six Eastern Partnership states. Ukraine became a pioneer country within the post-Soviet space for the DCFTA as part of an Association Agreement.[9] The Association Agreement would replace the Partnership and Cooperation Agreement and the EU–Ukraine Association Agenda replaces the Action Plan as an instrument of the European Neighborhood Policy. However, while the Association Agreement is symbolically important, it will not represent a breakthrough unless it mentions a membership perspective.

Even though Ukraine's ties to the EU have considerably strengthened over the past decade, the issue of Ukraine's EU membership remains a remote and uncertain perspective. The EU does not have any clear vision concerning the sequencing of its further enlargement. The 2011 Enlargement Strategy and Progress Report lists the countries with a perspective of accession in the future as Iceland, the Western Balkans and Turkey—but not Ukraine. The EU could not offer membership prospects to only Ukraine within the Eastern Partnership which is another stumbling block for Kyiv. Realistically Ukraine therefore does not have the possibility of receiving EU membership in the foreseeable future. Nevertheless, in order to facilitate and continue with the reform processes and strengthen pro-EU forces in Ukraine, it will be crucial to provide Ukraine with a clear European perspective through the attainment of realistic objectives.

---

[9] See L. Zsuzsa, "Troublesome triangle: The European Union, Russia and Their Common Post-Soviet Neighbourhood. The European Union's Eastern Partnership," *East European Studies*, No. 3. 2011, pp. 93-111.

Macro-Regional Integration

Ukraine has received new perspectives in its cooperation with the EU through macro-regional strategies that represent a new and promising answer by the EU to the growing number and diversity of member states. The Baltic Sea Strategy is a pilot project establishing the blueprint with the 'three no's' of no new institutions, no new legislation and no new funds. The new framework for regional cooperation could become popular with other member states not directly involved in the Baltic Sea region.

The next step was the Danube Strategy, which was adopted by the European Council at its June 2011 meeting at the end of the Hungarian Presidency. The Danube Strategy follows in the footprints of the Baltic Sea Strategy and unites eight EU member states and six regional neighbors of the EU, including Ukraine.

There is a potential third macro-region for the EU of the Adriatic Sea area that could include most of the Balkan states together with Italy and Greece. However, most of its potential members are, for the time being, not members of the EU.

All three macro-regions are located around important internal EU waterways: the Baltic Sea, the Danube River and Adriatic Sea and include most of the medium-sized and small EU member states. The 'circle of the big' and three macro-regions cover almost the entire territory of the EU (except Ireland and Portugal), together with countries that are within future enlargements and immediate neighborhood.

In the spirit of this new, macro-regional approach, Ukraine has two further opportunities for deepening and enriching its relations with the EU. Following the accession of Romania and Bulgaria and the launch of accession negotiations with Turkey, the EU has gained a potential dominant position in the Black Sea area. Two other 'giants'—Russia and Ukraine—are present and highly interested in that region. Furthermore, the Black Sea is directly connected with the South Caucasian area that possesses strategic importance for energy supplies to Europe. Instead of multi-vectoring between Russia and the EU, Ukraine should promote a complex 'win-win' strategy for the Black Sea region.

The second macro-regional opportunity for Ukraine is the economic potential of its Western region, Transcarpathia, which is surrounded by four EU member states, Poland, Slovakia, Hungary and Romania. All four countries and EU members are linked to Transcarpathia and each other through cultural, historical and ethnic ties. The Transcarpathian region could be developed into an EU bridgehead into Ukraine that would promote its integration into continental Europe. The region is already linked by broad-gauge railway to Hungary (Záhony) and Slovakia (Kosice) and its geographic location and multi-ethnic traditions are convenient as potential a offshore zone and for factories assembling products for the EU market.

Chapter Seven

Ukraine and Transatlantic Integration

F. Stephen Larrabee

The Orange Revolution inspired hopes both in Ukraine and in the West that Ukraine had turned an important corner politically and that the election of Viktor Yushchenko as president would lead to Ukraine's rapid integration into Euro-Atlantic institutions. However, Ukraine's integration into these institutions, especially NATO, has proven to be considerably more difficult than many in Ukraine and the West anticipated.

Several factors contributed to these difficulties. First, unlike in Eastern Europe, where NATO enjoyed a positive image, NATO had a negative image in Ukraine due to decades of anti-NATO propaganda by the Soviet authorities. As a result, popular support for NATO is much lower in Ukraine in comparison to other states in Central-Eastern Europe. For example, popular support for NATO is close to 80% in Poland and Romania, whereas in Ukraine it has hovered between 22-25%. Moreover, in the Russian-speaking areas of Eastern-Southern Ukraine it is below 10%.

Second, there was no consensus in the West about its policies toward Ukraine. While some countries, such as Poland and the United States, favored an active effort to support Ukraine's integration into Euro-Atlantic institutions, many European countries had doubts whether Ukraine was really an independent country and continued to view it, implicitly if not explicitly, lying within Russia's sphere of influence. This lack of unity inhibited the development of a coherent Western strategy toward Ukraine.

Finally, Russian opposition also played an important role. Ukraine's integration into Euro-Atlantic institutions—above all NATO—was seen in Moscow as representing a major strategic setback. In Russian eyes, it would alter the balance of power in Central-Eastern Europe to Russia's disadvantage and foreclose any residual possibility of building a "Slavic Union" of Russia, Ukraine and Belarus.

Psychologically, moreover, many Russians find it difficult to accept the idea of an independent Ukrainian state. The countries of Central-Eastern Europe had served as an important strategic buffer between Russia and 'Europe' during the Cold War. However, they were never part of Russian or Soviet territory (except for parts of Poland before 1918). Most of Ukraine, by contrast, had been an integral part of Russia and the Soviet Union for over three hundred years. Thus, psychologically, the loss of Ukraine was much harder for many Russians to accept and Russia has used various means, especially economic leverage, to inhibit Ukraine's closer integration into NATO.

Evolving Ukrainian Policy Toward NATO

Unlike most countries in Central-Eastern Europe, Ukraine did not initially aspire to become a member of NATO. In the early years after becoming independent, Ukraine pursued a non-aligned policy in part to avoid antagonizing Russia. Kyiv initially opposed NATO enlargement to Central-Eastern Europe because it feared that it would create new dividing lines in Europe and lead to increased Russian pressure on Ukraine. However, Moscow's hard-line opposition to NATO enlargement and Kyiv's desire to improve relations with the West contributed to a gradual shift in Ukraine's approach to enlargement. During 1995, Kyiv dropped its opposition to enlargement and began to regard the membership of Central-Eastern European countries, especially Poland, in NATO as giving security benefits for Ukraine as well.[1]

At the same time, under President Leonid Kuchma, Ukraine consciously began to strengthen ties to the Alliance. Ukraine was the first CIS state to join the Partnership for Peace (PfP) in January 1994, and it has been one of the most active participants in PfP exercises. At the

---

[1] For a detailed discussion on the shift in Ukraine's attitudes see F. Stephen Larrabee, "Ukraine's Place in European and Regional Security," in Lybornyr A. Hajda ed., *Ukraine in the World: Studies in International Relations and Security Structure of a Newly Independent State* (Cambridge, MA: Ukrainian Research Institute, Harvard University, 1998), pp. 249-270.

NATO summit in Madrid in July 1997, Kyiv signed the Charter on a Distinctive Partnership with NATO. Although the Charter did not provide explicit security guarantees, it called for the establishment of a crisis consultative mechanism that could be activated if Ukraine perceived a direct threat to its security.[2] This mechanism failed during the fall 2003 Tuzla crisis[3] when Ukraine tried to activate it.

The Charter also foresaw a broad expansion of ties between NATO and Ukraine in a number of key areas such as civil-military relations, democratic control of the armed forces, armaments cooperation, and defense planning. Thus, the Charter established a deeper relationship with Ukraine than with any non-NATO member—with the exception of Russia. Ukraine also built individual security relationships with Britain and the U.S.

The rapprochement with NATO was not undertaken because Ukraine felt a strong military threat. Rather it was part of a carefully calculated political balancing act pursued by Kuchma who sought to strengthen ties to NATO as a means of increasing his political leverage with Moscow.[4] Contrary to the concerns of many critics who feared that intensifying ties to NATO would lead to a sharp deterioration of relations with Russia, the rapprochement with NATO increased Ukraine's freedom of maneuver and led to an improvement of ties with Moscow. President Yeltsin's decision to sign the long-delayed Russian-Ukrainian Friendship and Cooperation Treaty in 1997 was in large part motivated by a desire to counter Ukraine's growing rapprochement with NATO. It reflected recognition by Yeltsin that his delaying tactics were driving Kyiv more strongly into the arms of the West.

---

[2] For the text of the Charter see "Charter On A Distinctive Partnership Between the North Atlantic Treaty Organization and Ukraine," *NATO Review*, Vol. 45, No. 4 (July-August 1997), Documentation Section. See also David Buchan and David White, "NATO signs charter with Ukraine," *Financial Times*, July 10, 1997.

[3] Tuzla lies to the West of the Crimea. In Fall 2003 Russia sought to build a dam connecting the North Caucasus to Tuzla. President Kuchma cut short a visit to Brazil and sent security forces to protect Ukraine's border.

[4] See F. Stephen Larrabee, "Ukraine's Balancing Act," *Survival*, Vol. 38, No. 2 (Summer 1996), pp. 143-165.

In May 2002, President Kuchma announced that Ukraine intended to abandon its policy of nonalignment and apply for NATO membership. Here again the decision was part of a calculated effort to counterbalance Russia. President Putin's decision to support the United States in the war on terrorism and the subsequent improvement in U.S.-Russian relations raised the prospect that Russia would have a closer relationship with NATO than Ukraine.

Ukraine's application for NATO membership was designed to undercut this prospect. However, Kuchma's increasingly repressive internal policies as well as suspicions that Ukraine had sold aircraft tracking systems to Iraq (the Kolchuga affair), led NATO to put relations with Ukraine on hold. The Alliance decided to wait until after the 2004 presidential elections before taking any new initiatives with Ukraine.

The Impact of the Orange Revolution

Yushchenko's election as president in December 2004 opened a new stage in Ukraine's relations with NATO. In an attempt to encourage Yushchenko's pro-Western reform course, NATO offered Ukraine Intensified Dialogue status in April 2005—a preparatory step toward an individualized Membership Action Plan (MAP). By the spring of 2006, there were widespread expectations that Ukraine would be offered MAP at the NATO summit in Riga (November 2006), with a possible membership invitation in 2008 leading to full membership in 2010-2012.

However, the collapse of the Orange Coalition in the summer of 2006 and Yanukovych's return to power as prime minister dashed these hopes. During a trip to

Brussels in September 2006 Yanukovych withdrew Ukraine's support for MAP and the issue became a dead letter until after September 2007 pre-term elections that resulted in a victory of the Orange Coalition.

One of the first acts of the new Ukrainian government, headed by Prime Minister Yulia Tymoshenko, was to revive Ukraine's application for MAP. In January 2008, Tymoshenko, Yushchenko, and Rada (Parliament) Chairman Arseniy Yatseniuk sent a letter to NATO seeking a MAP and NATO membership at the Bucharest summit. Ukraine's request for a MAP along with that of Georgia touched off a lively debate within the Alliance in the run up to the NATO summit in Bucharest in April 2008. President Bush pushed hard for the Alliance to grant Ukraine and Georgia MAP status, which was viewed by many, especially the Russian leadership, as being a precursor to NATO membership. France and Germany, however, opposed the idea, fearing that it would undercut any hope of an improvement in NATO's relations with Russia.

As Ronald Asmus has noted, the debate over MAP at Bucharest was not just a debate about Ukraine and Georgia's technical performance and whether they met the loose standards set down in NATO doctrine. It was really a debate about the future of enlargement and more generally about relations with Russia.[5] Those who opposed granting Georgia and Ukraine a MAP did so not only because they doubted whether Georgia and Ukraine were really prepared for NATO membership, but also because they feared granting Georgia and Ukraine a MAP would be the first step down a slippery slope they could not control and which threatened to strain NATO's cohesion and relations with Moscow.

The Bucharest summit ended with a confusing compromise. France and Germany succeeded in blocking the granting of MAP to Ukraine and Georgia. However, the communiqué issued at the end of the summit by the NATO Heads of State and Governments stated that Ukraine and Georgia would one day be admitted to NATO, although no specific date or timetable was mentioned.

Thus, from Moscow's point of view the outcome was even worse than the Russian leadership had expected. Ukraine and Georgia had been denied MAP but had been given a formal commitment that they would one day become members of the Alliance.

---

[5] See Ronald D. Asmus, *A Little War That Shook The World* (New York: Palgrave Macmillan, 2010), p. 117.

The Changing International
Context for Ukrainian Membership

The Bucharest summit marked the high-water mark of Ukraine's advance toward NATO membership. Since the summit, prospects for Ukraine's entry into NATO have declined. Several factors contributed to pushing the issue of Ukrainian membership in NATO off the international agenda for the immediate future.

The first was the Russo-Georgian war in August 2008. The Russian invasion of Georgia was a sharp reminder that power politics still mattered and underscored that Russia was prepared to defend its interests in the post-Soviet space with force, if necessary. The invasion made clear that Russia was still a power to be reckoned with and that any attempt to promote security interests in the post-Soviet space would need to take Russian security concerns more directly into consideration.

At the same time, it underscored the limits of American power. Faced with a Kremlin determined to defend its interests in a region that Moscow regarded as part of its sphere of 'privileged interests,' the United States could do little but utter meek verbal protests. When push came to shove, few NATO members—including the United States—had much stomach for a military confrontation with Russia over Georgia. Moreover, the Russian invasion raised fears that South Ossetia could be a trial run for an attempt by Moscow to raise territorial claims on Crimea, especially in light of Putin's remark at the Bucharest summit that Ukraine was an "artificial entity."[6]

In short, the invasion of Georgia had a sobering impact on Western thinking about the modalities and wisdom of NATO's enlargement into the post-Soviet space. In the aftermath of the invasion, the issue of NATO membership for Ukraine and Georgia was put on indefinite hold. While the door to NATO membership remains open to Ukraine (and Georgia) in principle, in reality there is little support in Western capitals for further enlargement of the Alliance in the near term, especially as long as Yanukovych remains Ukraine's president.

---

[6] See Taras Kuzio, *The Crimea. Europe's Next Flashpoint?* (Washington DC: Jamestown Foundation, November 2010).

Western relations with the East, in fact, appear to be entering a new phase. For the past two decades, enlargement has been the main vehicle for promoting stability and security eastward in both NATO and the EU. But as Bruce Jackson has noted, this "go-go period" of NATO expansion to the East has ended. [7] Macedonia and perhaps Serbia may at some point become NATO members. However, further enlargement of the Alliance into the post-Soviet space has essentially been put on hold.

Within the EU as well, the momentum behind enlargement has slowed visibly in the last few years. The top EU priority since 2006 has been ensuring ratification of the Lisbon Treaty and other major initiatives have been subordinated to that goal. As a consequence, there has been little active support for new initiatives aimed at further enlargement and in effect, further enlargement to the East has been put on hold.

The Eastern Partnership—the EU's main policy instrument for dealing with countries on its eastern periphery—emphasizes trade and soft power as instruments for fostering closer ties to the countries in the western periphery of the post-Soviet space. However, unlike the association agreements with the states of the Western Balkans, the Eastern Partnership does not offer a prospect of membership. Ukraine's Association Agreement with the EU likewise differed from the Association Agreements signed in the 1990s with Central-Eastern Europe, which contains a commitment to eventual membership. Ukraine's Association Agreement contained no such commitment.

With neither NATO nor EU membership on the horizon the only vehicle for keeping open the prospect for Ukraine's closer ties to Euro-Atlantic institution is the Deep Comprehensive Free Trade Agreement (DCFTA) being negotiated between Ukraine and the EU. However, that agreement could be frozen due to concerns in various EU member states about political repression and serious violations of rule of law—particularly the arrest and trial of former prime minister Yulia Tymoshenko—that have occurred since President Yanukovych

---

[7] Bruce Pitcairn Jackson, "A Turning Point for Europe's East," *Policy Review*, No. 160 (April-May 2010), pp. 49-61.

took office. Following her sentence in October 2011 to seven years imprisonment the EU cancelled a visit to Brussels by Yanukovych and it remains unclear if the negotiations towards the signing of an Association Agreement will be completed. Most certainly, even if it was signed, the Association Agreement would not be ratified by the European Parliament, which issued a damning resolution on October 28, 2011, and 27 EU members parliaments.

U.S. Policy

At the same time, U.S. policy toward the post-Soviet space has shifted in small but important ways. The Bush Administration pursued an active policy towards the western periphery of the post-Soviet space. Along with Georgia, Ukraine was seen as poster child for the administration's democracy promotion program as both countries underwent color revolutions in 2003-2004. As noted earlier, Bush strongly supported awarding MAP status to Ukraine and Georgia at the 2006 Riga and 2008 Bucharest summits.

The Obama Administration, by contrast, has been much more cautious and circumspect in its approach to the expansion of Western interests into the western periphery of the post-Soviet space. While the door to Georgian and Ukrainian membership in NATO has been kept open rhetorically, in practice membership for both countries has been put on hold and subordinated to the Obama administration's effort to 'reset' relations with Moscow.

In addition, the democratic revolutions in the Middle East have diverted attention away from the CIS. With the Middle East in turmoil, Washington has been forced to focus increasing attention on trying to stabilize the Middle East and has had less time to pay attention to developments in the CIS. The EU, in turn, has been increasingly preoccupied with fallout from the sovereign debt crisis and the crisis surrounding the euro.

The Obama Administration's more cautious policy toward NATO enlargement has brought U.S. policy more in line with European policy. At the same time, it has generated concerns among some Central-Eastern European allies, particularly Poland and the Baltic states, that the United States is losing interest in promoting democracy and reform in the western periphery of the post-Soviet space.[8]

However, the Obama reset policy does not mean that the United States is abandoning support for democracy and reform in Ukraine and the western periphery of the post-Soviet space.[9] This is clearly seen in the strong U.S. condemnation of selective justice and of Tymoshenko's sentence. U.S. officials have repeatedly stressed that the United States does not accept the idea of "spheres of influence." Indeed, "completing Europe"—that is, extending stability, security, prosperity and democracy to the entire European continent—is one of the explicit goals of the Obama Administration's European policy.

Yanukovych's Election: Back to the Future

The third—and most important—factor influencing the issue of Ukrainian membership in NATO has been the change in Ukrainian policy under President Yanukovych. When Yanukovych was elected in February 2010, many observers expected that he would pursue a "multi vector" policy similar to the one pursued by President Kuchma that sought to balance relations with Russia with good ties to the West.

However, these expectations proved to be wrong. In his first two years in office, Yanukovych has pursued a series of policies that have exacerbated internal divisions, diminished the prospects for closer ties to the West, and reduced Ukraine's freedom of maneuver. This has left

---

[8] This unease was reflected in an Open Letter to President Obama in the autumn of 2009 signed by a distinguished group of Central and East European intellectuals and former officials, including former Polish President Lech Walesa and Vaclav Havel, former president of the Czech Republic. For the text of the letter, see "An Open Letter to the Obama Administration from Central and Eastern Europe," *Radio Free Europe*, July 16, 2009. Available at: http://www.rferl.org/content/An_Open_Letter_ To_The_Obama_Administration_From_Central_and_Eastern_Europe/1778449.html. Also see Pavol Demes, Istvan Gyarmati, Ivan Krastev, Kadri Ljik, Adam Rotfeld, and Alexandra Vondra, "Why the Obama Administration should not take Central and Eastern Europe for Granted" (Washington DC: German Marshall Fund of the United States, July 15, 2009).

[9] For a more skeptical view of Obama's reset policy, see Taras Kuzio, "Obama's Russia-Reset Masks the Fact that Eurasia Including Ukraine, Is No Longer a US Strategic Priority," *Ukrainian Analyst*, Vol.3, No.4 (January 31, 2011).

Ukraine more isolated internationally and created the conditions for Kyiv's potential drift back into the Russian economic and political orbit.

In April 2010, the Stability and Reforms coalition headed by Yanukovych railroaded through parliament a 25-year extension of the existing twenty year agreement (signed in 1997) allowing Russia to base the Black Sea Fleet in Sevastopol until 2042-2047. The agreement was ratified without proper parliamentary oversight and in violation of a constitutional provision forbidding foreign bases on Ukrainian territory. It provoked a virtual riot in the parliament and led to fist fights between members, the hurling of eggs and igniting of smoke bombs. In return for extending the base agreement, Russia agreed to lower the price of imported gas by 30 percent. However, due to the falling demand for gas, Russia had already begun renegotiating contracts in Europe and giving customers discounts. Thus, the 30 percent discount simply brought the price negotiated with Yanukovych down to current European average prices.

Moreover, the gas agreement reduces the incentive for Ukraine to reform its inefficient and corrupt energy sector, and commits the country to buying more gas in subsequent years than it may need. At the same time, it increases Ukraine's economic and energy dependence on Russia, strengthening Kyiv's single-vector foreign policy.

In summer 2010, Yanukovych withdrew Ukraine's support for NATO membership—a policy he had not opposed as Prime Minister in Kuchma's cabinet in 2002-2004. A July 2010 law on foreign policy described Ukraine henceforth as a "non-bloc" country. However, it remains unclear how Ukraine can be a neutral country while having a long-term foreign (i.e., Russian) base on its soil. In addition, the term "non-bloc" is a throw back to the Cold War and fails to take into account that the EU is an emerging bloc seeking to develop its own security and defense policy (ESDP).

In practical terms, Ukraine's withdrawal of its support for NATO membership does not mean much since there is little support within NATO for admitting Ukraine in the near future. Routine PfP cooperation with NATO has continued but any progress toward membership will have to await the election of a more democratic government in Kyiv committed to genuine reform and Euro-Atlantic integration.

On the domestic front, there has been a clear step back from democratic practices under Yanukovych, especially trials of opposition leaders, that threatens to jeopardize negotiations on the DCFTA.[10] Corruption has visibly increased which is having an economic impact. Foreign direct investment is falling and the European Union has currently frozen $100 million of financial assistance as a direct result of the administration's failure to curb graft in public-sector procurement. Harassment of opposition parties has also been stepped up. The most egregious example is the arrest and sent former Prime Minister Tymoshenko, who was accused of abuse of office and was sentenced to a seven years in prison in a trial that was clearly politically motivated. The sentence led to a storm of protests from the US, Canada, EU and EU members.

A Western Policy for the Long Haul: Toward an "Open Ukraine" in the Euro-Atlantic Community

Against the background of these changes since Yanukovych's election in February 2010 Western policymakers may be tempted to write off Ukraine and turn their attention elsewhere. However, this would be a strategic mistake. The United States and the EU have a strong stake in keeping open a European and Transatlantic orientation for Ukraine. A reorientation of Ukrainian policy toward Russia would shift the strategic balance in Europe and have a negative impact on the prospects for democratic change on Europe's eastern periphery, making it much more difficult for Georgia and Moldova to pursue their pro-Western course. It would also have a dampening impact on the long-term prospects for reform in Belarus by creating an eastern Slavic bloc of nations suspicious of the West.

While it is difficult to predict Ukraine's political trajectory, the United States and EU need to take the long view. Ukraine, like Turkey, is in the midst of an identity crisis which will have a profound impact on the country's political evolution. This struggle is between Ukraine's eastern orientation, promoted by elites in the Russified east-

---

[10]For a detailed analysis of the backsliding see the annual report, *Freedom in the World 2011* (Washington D.C.: Freedom House, 2011). See also Vaclav Havel, "Ukraine is Losing its Way," *Moscow Times*, August 31, 2011.

ern parts of Ukraine, and a western orientation advocated by the pro-western elites in Central and Western Ukraine. This identity crisis is likely to take time to sort out.

Economic and oligarchic elites around Yanukovych fear Russian economic domination and prefer the DCFTA to the CIS Customs Union. At the same time, they want to have their cake and eat it too by enjoying the economic benefits from the economic and trade provisions of the DCFTA while simultaneously undertaking policies at home that violate European values and seek to establish political and economic monopolization of power. This attempt to combine a type of Ukrainian "Putinism" at home with European integration abroad has nearly derailed the Association Agreement and DCFTA and threatens to hamper its ratification.

As Ukraine struggles to define its identity and find its place in the new European security order, the door to Europe should be kept open to Ukraine. U.S. and European policy should be aimed at strengthening democratic institutions and promoting the growth of civil society, especially an independent media, and business and student exchanges. As Bohdan Vitvitsky shows in his chapter, rule of law and corruption issues are central to the emergence of an "Open Ukraine."

While the door to NATO membership for Ukraine should be kept open in principle, the issue of NATO membership is likely to remain on the back burner for the immediate future. Focusing on NATO membership now will only inflame the political atmosphere and make progress in other important areas more difficult. The main obstacle is not Russian opposition—though this is an important factor—but low public support for Ukrainian membership. As long as only about a quarter of the population favors membership, the prospect for Ukraine being admitted to NATO will remain remote. With a more democratic and Western-oriented political leadership in power, support for Ukraine's integration into Euro-Atlantic institutions—especially NATO—could increase. But changing Ukrainian attitudes toward NATO will take time. However, until there is stronger support for NATO among the Ukrainian population, the question of Ukrainian membership in NATO will remain largely theoretical rather than an important issue on the political agenda.

While Ukrainian membership in NATO is not feasible for the time being, other steps in the security field could be taken to strengthen Ukraine's ties to the Euro-Atlantic community. The United States and its European allies should seek to engage the Ukrainian military in a dialogue on military reform and continue to involve Ukraine in peace-keeping operations, both within NATO and on a bilateral basis. Nuclear safety is another area where the United States and Ukraine could usefully increase cooperation. With growing "Putinization" of the security forces, their democratic control is an important area for policy makers in NATO and NATO member governments to focus on. Greater emphasis should be placed on democratic control of the internal security forces (Interior Ministry and Security Service) that have been used as the vanguard for the growing authoritarianism.

The main objective of such contacts and dialogue should be to strengthen cooperation in areas where there is mutual interest while encouraging progress toward establishing more open democratic institutions. In many cases, this may not necessarily involve highly visible projects but rather efforts to enhance cooperation at the grass roots level. The goal should be to strengthen ties that can lead to the emergence of a more pluralistic and democratic Ukraine *over the medium-long run*.

This is particularly important in light of the election of Vladimir Putin as the next president of Russia in the March 2012 Russian presidential elections. Putin's election could result in a toughening of Russian policy toward Ukraine, especially in the economic area. Such a situation could provide new opportunities to engage the Ukrainian leadership and strengthen Ukraine's ties to the Euro-Atlantic community. While Yanukovych favors strong ties to Russia, he does not want Ukraine to become a Russian satellite or himself a Russian *gubernator*. Nor do the Ukrainian oligarchs who are an important interest group within the Yanukovych administration.

Indeed, there are already signs of growing differences between Ukraine and Russia in the economic area. These could increase under Putin. If they do, Yanukovych could begin to show greater interest in closer ties to the West—especially Europe—in order to counterbalance ties with and pressure from Moscow, as Kuchma did.

Whether Yanukovych has the political skill to pursue such a policy is far from clear. But if he shows an interest in trying, the United States and the EU should be ready to engage him while at the same time continuing to push for more comprehensive economic and political reforms aimed at facilitating Ukraine's integration into Euro-Atlantic institutions.

About the Authors

Péter Balázs is Professor at the Budapest Corvinus University and the Central European University (CEU) as well as Director of the CEU's EU Enlargement Center. An economist and diplomat by training, he was Minister of Foreign Affairs of Hungary from in 2009 to 2010. In 2002, he was appointed Secretary of State for Integration and Foreign Economic Policy. In 2004, he held the position of EU Commissioner for Regional Policy.

Daniel Hamilton is the Austrian Marshall Plan Foundation Professor and Director of the Center for Transatlantic Relations at Johns Hopkins University's School of Advanced International Studies. He also serves as Executive Director of the American Consortium for EU Studies, designated by the European Commission as the EU Center of Excellence Washington, DC. He has held a variety of senior positions in the U.S. Department of State, including Deputy Assistant Secretary for European Affairs, responsible for NATO, OSCE and transatlantic security issues; U.S. Special Coordinator for Southeast European Stabilization; Associate Director of the Secretary of State's Policy Planning Staff; and Director for Policy in the Bureau of European Affairs. In 2008 he served as the first Robert Bosch Foundation Senior Diplomatic Fellow in the German Foreign Office. He has also taught at the Hertie School of Governance in Berlin, the University of Innsbruck and the Free University of Berlin. Recent publications include *Europe's Economic Crisis* (2011); *Preventing Conflict, Managing Crisis: European and American Perspectives* (2011); *Transatlantic 2020: A Tale of Four Futures* (2011); *Europe 2020: Competitive or Complacent?* (2011); *Shoulder to Shoulder: Forging a Strategic U.S.-EU Partnership* (2010), *Alliance Reborn: An Atlantic Compact for the 21st Century* (2009); *The Transatlantic Economy* (annual editions, 2004-2011); *The Wider Black Sea Region: Strategic, Economic and Energy Perspectives* (2008), *The New Eastern Europe: Ukraine, Belarus and Moldova* (2007), and *Terrorism and International Relations* (2006).

Oleksiy Haran is professor of political science at the University of 'Kyiv-Mohyla Academy.' He is the author of *Ukraine in Europe: Ques-*

tions and Answers (2009), *Kill the Dragon: History of the RUKH (Movement)* and *New Parties in Ukraine* (1993). He was co-editor of *Emerging Authorities in Ukraine* (1997), *Ukrainian Left: Between Leninism and Social Democracy* (2000), and *Economic and Political Transformation in Russia and Ukraine* (2003). He has been Ukraine Editor of the yearbook *Nations in Transit* published by Freedom House. He has been a visiting professor and guest lecturer at Harvard University, Columbia University, University of California-Berkeley, Stanford University, Carnegie Endowment for International Peace, RAND, and the Brookings Institution. He has published monographs for the Harvard Kennedy School, Center for Strategic and International Studies, and Federal Institute for Eastern Studies (Cologne).

Taras Kuzio is a Visiting Professor in the Slavic Research Center, Hokkaido University and Non-Resident Fellow at the Center for Transatlantic Relations, School of Advanced International Studies, John Hopkins University. Previously, he was an inaugural Austrian Marshall Plan Foundation Fellow at CTR. He has been a Visiting Professor at the Institute for European, Russian and Eurasian Studies, Elliott School of International Affairs, George Washington University and Senior Research Fellow in the Centre for Russian and East European Studies at the University of Birmingham. He has also served as Head of Mission of the NATO Information and Documentation Centre in Kyiv. He is the author and editor of 14 books, including *Theoretical and Comparative Perspectives on Nationalism* (2007) and *Ukraine-Crimea-Russia: Triangle of Conflict* (2007). He is the author of 5 think tank monographs, 25 book chapters, and author of 60 scholarly articles on post-communist and Ukrainian politics, nationalism and European security. He has guest edited 6 special issues of *Communist and Post-Communist Studies, Problems of Post-Communism, East European Politics and Society, Nationalities Papers* and *Journal of Ukrainian Studies.* Taras Kuzio received a BA in Economics from the University of Sussex, an MA in Soviet and Eastern European Studies from the University of London and a PhD in Political Science from the University of Birmingham, England. He was a Post-Doctoral Fellow at Yale University.

Serhiy Kudelia is a Visiting Fellow at the Elliott School of International Affairs, George Washington University and a professorial lecturer at Johns Hopkins University-SAIS. He has held teaching and research positions at the University of Toronto and National University 'Kyiv-Mohyla Academy.' He served as an advisor to the Deputy Prime Minister of Ukraine in 2008-2009. His articles have appeared in the *Journal of Communist Studies and Transition Politics* and *Communist and Post-Communist Studies* and in the edited volume *Orange Revolution and Aftermath: Mobilization, Apathy and the State in Ukraine (2010)*. He is co-author of *The Strategy of Campaigning: Lessons from Ronald Reagan and Boris Yeltsin (2007)* with Kiron Skinner, Bruce Bueno de Mesquita and Condoleezza Rice. Serhiy Kudelia received an MA in political science from Stanford University and a PhD in international relations from Johns Hopkins University-SAIS.

F. Stephen Larrabee holds the Distinguished Chair in European Security at the Washington DC office of the Rand Corporation. Before joining RAND, he served as vice president and director of studies of the Institute of East–West Security Studies in New York from 1983 to 1989. He was a distinguished Scholar in Residence at the Institute from 1989 to 1990. From 1978 to 1981, he served on the U.S. National Security Council staff in the White House as a specialist on Soviet–East European affairs and East-West political-military relations. His recent RAND monographs include *Troubled Partnership: U.S.-Turkish Relations in an Era of Global Geopolitical Change* (2010); *Turkey as a U.S. Security Partner* (2008); *The Rise of Political Islam in Turkey* (with Angel Rabasa, 2008); and *Encouraging Trade and Foreign Direct Investment in Ukraine* (with Keith Crane, 2007). Recent articles include 'Arming Europe,' in *The National Interest* (with Seth G. Jones, Winter 2005–2006); and 'ESDP and NATO: Assuring Complementarity,' in *The International Spectator* (January–March 2004). In addition, he is the coauthor (with Julian Lindley-French) of *Revitalizing the Transatlantic Security Partnership: An Agenda for Action* (RAND/Bertelsmann Stiftung, 2008); the editor of *The Volatile Powder Keg: Balkan Security After the Cold War* (American University Press, 1994); and co-editor (with Robert Blackwill) of *Conventional Arms Control and East-West Security* (Duke University Press. He holds a B.A., Amherst College, M.I.A. in international affairs, Columbia University; and Ph.D. in political science, Columbia University.

Marcin Święcicki has been an economist, government minister, Mayor (President) of Warsaw from 1994-1999, parliamentarian and city councillor. He has been an adviser to the Lithuanian President, United Nations Blue Ribbon Commissions and the United Nations

Development Program (UNDP). He was Director of Economic and Environmental Affairs at the Organization for Security and Cooperation in Europe (OSCE) in 2002-2005. From 1972 to 1989 he worked in various economic capacities in the Polish government and from 1989 to 1991 was Minister for Foreign Economic Cooperation in the Tadeusz Mazowiecki government, where he signed Poland's first agreement with the European Union. He was an activist in the Catholic Intelligentsia Club (1965-1972) and Union of Socialist Youth (1969-1979). Marcin Święcicki has received a BA, MA and PhD in Economics from the University of Warsaw and has been a Visiting Professor at Harvard University and George Washington University.

Frank Umbach is Senior Associate of the Centre for European Security Strategies (CESS) in Munich-Berlin and a Consultant on International Energy Security. From 1996-2007, he was the Head of the 'International Energy Security' and 'Security Policies in Asia-Pacific' programs at the German Council on Foreign Relations (DGAP) in Berlin. Since February 2007 he has been an official advisor to the Lithuanian government on international energy security. He is also Co-Chair of the European Committee of the Council for Security Cooperation in Asia-Pacific (ESCSCAP/CSCAP-Europe) and a member of two expert groups on transatlantic energy security. He was a research fellow at the Federal Institute for East European and International Affairs (BIOst) in Cologne (1991-1994) and at the Japanese Foreign Ministry's Institute for International Affairs (1995-1996). He was a Research Assistant in the Office of the 'Special Advisor for Central and East European Affairs,' Office of the General Secretary of NATO, in Brussels. He studied Political Science, East European history and international law at the universities of Marburg and Bonn, and received his Ph.D. in Bonn. He has been a consultant to the German Foreign and Defense Ministries. Frank Umbach is the author of more than 200 publications, including *Global Energy Security: Strategic Challenges for the European and German Foreign Policy* (2003); *Cooperation or Conflict in Asia- Pacific? China's Tying into Regional Security Structures and the Implications for Europe* (2003); and *The Red Alliance. Development and Decay of the Warsaw Pact 1955-1991* (2005).

Bohdan Vitvitsky is a U.S. federal prosecutor and legal adviser for the U.S. Department of Justice in Ukraine. In 2007–09 he was the Resident Legal Advisor at the U.S. Embassy in Kyiv, focusing on the rule of law and corruption issues. He has written and lectured on law, philosophy and history. Bohdan Vitvitsky is the founder of the Ukrainian American Professionals and Businesspersons Association of New York and New Jersey. He holds a Juris Doctor and a PhD in philosophy from Columbia University.